ACHIEVEMENT MOTIVATION AND ACHIEVEMENT IN ENGLISH OF SCHOOL STUDENTS

ACHIEVEMENT MOTIVATION AND ACHIEVEMENT IN ENGLISH OF SCHOOL STUDENTS

By

M. Jyosthana

M.A. (Litt.), M.Ed., M.Phil.
Lecturer in English
R.V.R. College of Elementary Teacher Education
JKC College Road, Choudarypeta
Guntur — 522 006
(Andhra Pradesh)

Editor

Dr. Digumarti Bhaskara Rao

M.Sc., M.A., M.A., M.Ed., Ph.D.
Principal & Research Director
R.V.R. College of Education
D-43 (277) S.V.N. Colony
Guntur — 522 006
&
Member, Board of Studies in Education
Acharya Nagarjuna University
digumartibhaskararao@rediffmail.com

DISCOVERY PUBLISHING HOUSE PVT. LTD.
NEW DELHI-110 002

Published by:
Tilak Wasan
DISCOVERY PUBLISHING HOUSE PVT. LTD.
4383/4A, Ansari Road, Darya Ganj
New Delhi-110 002 (India)
Phone : +91-11-23279245, 43596064-65
Fax : +91-11-23253475
E-mail : parul.wasan@gmail.com
discoverypublishinghouse@gmail.com
web : www.discoverypublishinggroup.com

***First Edition:* 2012**
ISBN: 978-93-5056-002-0

Achievement Motivation and Achievement in English of School Students

Printed at:
Shree Balaji Art Press
Delhi

Dedicated
to the Beloved Family of My GURU

Mr. Digumarti Bhaskara Rao, Mrs. Pushpa Latha
Ms. Harshitha, Mr. Sai Krishna

Preface

English deserves to be regarded as a world language of all the languages in the world and hence it is considered as the most important language in the world today. Whatever important developments that have happened in the last two hundred years, the English-speaking people did them. So, any person who wants to become knowledgeable by becoming part of those human developments must learn English. Considering the importance of English language today, English is made one of the compulsory languages of learning in the schools throughout the world.

Achievement motivation is the desire of a person to meet certain standards of excellence. Academic achievement is one's learning attainments, accomplishments or proficiencies in performing a given task in education. Achievement in English refers to the accomplishment in English examination.

The secondary school students are holding high achievement motivation. There is a significant difference in the achievement motivation of rural and urban school students, government and private school students, and reserved and unreserved caste students, except in boys and girls where there is no significant difference in their achievement motivation. The secondary school students are possessing high achievement in English. There is no significant difference in the achievement in English between boys and girls, government and private school students, and reserved and unreserved caste students, except in rural and urban school students where there is a significant difference between them. There is a very low positive correlation between achievement motivation and achievement in English in secondary school students. The correlation between achievement motivation and achievement in English is positive at middle level; is positive at a very low level in boys, urban students, government school students, private school students, reserved caste students and unreserved caste students and is negative at a very low level in rural students.

The students should have high achievement motivation to get high achievement in English. For this, the teachers and the parents should provide ample opportunities for fair learning of English and do well in English examinations.

Dr. Digumarti Bhaskara Rao
digumartibhaskararao@rediffmail.com
Tele-Mobile: +91 949 3333 555

Contents

1 Introduction

Mahatma Gandhi, the Father of India, stated that Education is drawing out of the best in child and man — body, mind and spirit". Swami Vivekananda explained that "Education is the manifestation of the perfection that is already in man". According to John Dewey "Education is the development of all those capacities in the individual, which will enable him to control his environment and fulfill his possibilities".

Teaching and Learning

The purpose of teaching is to help pupils to learn. Each pupil learns, however, from his own efforts and experiences. A teacher may inspire a student to what to learn and may guide him in experiences from which he may learn some fact, attitude or skill, but the teacher cannot learn it for him. Each individual must learn for himself.

A good teacher can play important roles in the learning of an individual. He can observe the individual and try to understand his present abilities, interests and needs, stimulate and encourage him to explore them further and help to provide further experiences of such a nature as he can probably use in satisfying the needs and curiosities he feels at the moment. The effective teacher is an artist at guiding a student's experiences in ways that will satisfy, at least in part, some of the needs he feels at that time what a particular individual actually learns from and experiences may be quite different from the things his teacher had expected him to learn. The new knowledge or interest gained by a person through an experience is always an outgrowth of his previous concepts and interests, rather than the particular growth that the teacher had hoped the experience might stimulate.

Teaching and learning at the high school and college level are not essentially different in their fundamental nature and relationships from teaching and learning at the elementary school level. Older learners have usually developed, however, certain habits and abilities that were not strong in earlier years. Older children have usually learned, for example, to sit still for longer periods of time. They have often learned to find certain kinds of information for themselves by turning to the dictionary or to other sources of information. Most of them have learned to depend more on themselves and less on what the teacher or textbook says for finding satisfactory answers to the questions in their minds.

The most effective teachers, in high school and colleges as well as in the primary grades, are artists in recognizing, encouraging and developing the normal desires of young persons to understand and make intelligent use of the things that appear to concern them. An artist teacher can recognize and nourish a student's desire to develop more adequate understandings, even though the particular concern of the student at the moment may not be a part of the limited subject that the teacher was employed to teach.

Teaching of English

"One hundred and fifty years of intimate contact has made English an integral part of our educational system and this cannot be changed without injury to the cause of education in India. In addition, English has today become

one of the major languages of the world and Indians can neglect its study only at the risk of loss to them."
—*Jawaharlal Nehru, former Prime Minister of India*

English is the most important language in the world today, whatever important developments that have happened in the last two hundred years; the English-speaking people did them. The English speaking countries developed most of modern technology. So, any country that wants to become rich by using technology must learn English.

Of all the languages in the world today, English deserves to be regarded as a world language. It is the first language of U.K., U.S.A., Canada and Australia. It is spoken and read by many millions of Europeans, Africans, Chinese, Indians, Japanese, South Africans, etc., as a second language.

English language is the common means of communication between people of different nations. According to F.G. French, "Because of rapid spread of industrial development, science and technology, international trade and commerce and the close interdependence of nations, English has become a world language".

India become aware of a language called English with the advent of the British from England. English is a rich and beautiful language, which can't be compared to any other Indian languages. It has become the queen of all languages in India.

Motivation

In order to make learning in the subject meaningful, it is necessary that the students are motivated before they are made to learn anything. A strong interest can be aroused and whole-hearted attention to the extent of concentration can be secured through proper motivation.

Motivation is the basic activity for creating interest through various means such as aids, relationships, historical references, anecdotes, possible applications, and games.

Emphasizing the importance of motivation in the learning process, Kelly has stated, "Motivation is the central factor in the effective management of the process of learning. Some type of motivation must be present in all learning."

Motivation, in its psychological sense, is concerned with the inculcation and stimulation of the learner's interest in the learning activities. It makes a student interested in his studies. It is the force, which energizes a man to act and to make constant efforts in order to satisfy his basic motives.

Tremendous research has been done on the psychology of motivation in the last 70 years or so and a number of new theories have been evolved to explain human behaviour. K.B. Madson is his book 'Theory of Motivation' has given twenty-four theories of motivation that propose different explanations of human behaviour. Historically, the word 'motivation' comes from the Latin root 'movers', which means to move. Thus, we can say that, in its literal meaning, motivation is the process of arousing movement in the organism. The movement is produced and regulated through the release of energy in the individual.

The activating forces for the motivation may be termed as needs, drives or motives. Needs are general wants or desires and are said to be the very basis of behaviour. They can be broadly classified as biological needs and socio-psychological needs. Biological needs include all the bodily or organic needs such as the need for oxygen, food, water, rest, sleep and sex and the like. They are linked with the survival of the organism and the species. Socio-psychological needs, like the need for love and affection, security, affiliation, self-assertion and self-actualization, are linked with the socio-cultural environment and psychological makeup of an individual. They are considered essential as their deprivation may seriously affect the survival and welfare of an individual.

A need gives rise to a drive that activates an individual from within and directs his activities to a goal that may bring about the satisfaction of the need. Biological needs give birth to biological drives such as hunger, thirst and sex, and the socio-psychological needs produce socio-psychological drives such as fear, anxiety, approval and achievement drives. Drives are also influenced and guided by incentives like praise, appreciation, reward, bonus, etc., as reinforcing agents.

The word 'drive' has, now-a-days, been replaced by the more forceful term 'motive'. It is defined as an energetic force or tendency (learned or innate) working within the individual to compel, persuade or inspire him to act for the satisfaction of his basic needs or attainment of some specific purposes.

Psychologists have identified and named a number of motives. Hunger motive primarily arises from our body's need for food and the thirst motive from the need for fluid. The need for food or fluid is conveyed to the brain which in turn produces the motivation behaviour involving hunger or thirst. Apart from the biological function, the hunger and the thirst motives are also controlled by personal experiences and social learning. The sex motives, although not as essential for an individual's survival as food and water, constitute a highly powerful psycho-physical motive. The material motive is stimulated both by biological factors and social learning.

Motives like the aggression motive, the affiliation motive and the achievement motive are purely learned as they are linked with the demands of one's environment in terms of social learning.

While curiosity can be considered as an immediate and autotelic motivation as it is immediately reinforcing and this reinforcement lies in the interaction between person and task (in uncertainty reduction). Motivation can be also considered as an extended person-intrinsic motivation because its reinforcement is delayed and arises from an interaction within the person. The motivation is a pattern of planning of actions and of feelings connected with striving to achieve some internalized standard of excellence, as contrasted, for example with power or friendship.

Need for Achievement

Over the time, the individual assesses his or her behaviour and evaluates the result. Achievement motivation is called need for achievement (n-Ach). Important here is the attitude to achieve rather than the achievements themselves.

The need to achieve appears to be a need that becomes part of an individual's personality and affects that person's behaviour in every facet of life including education. Individuals with high need for achievement are people interested in excellence for its own sake rather than for the extrinsic rewards it can bring such as money or prestige. They prefer situations in which their personal responsibility affects the outcome. They tend to prefer to control their destinies and to make independent judgments based on their own education and experiences. They choose challenging goals (McClelland, 1958) and prefer delayed, large rewards to immediate and smaller rewards.

Educationally, work is used for achievement and achievement has been sparse and only moderately successful. It was demonstrated that under some circumstances high need-for-achievement people would persist longer at a challenging task. Challenge, especially that of marks or grades in school, has been investigated: but since need-for-achievement is considered to be an intrinsic motivator and independent of external reinforces such as grades and prizes, it cannot be expected that there should be a high correlation between it and school achievement.

Since need-for-achievement is regarded as learned motivation, training programmes have been developed for children to enhance their levels of it, and encouraging findings have demonstrated that even though academic grades may not have improved greatly, purposeful planning and action in many phases of life have resulted.

The conditions under which achievement motives best develop require that learners—

- can give reasons for developing a given motive
- understand that the motive is realistic
- can link the motive to deeds and daily events in life
- commit themselves to concrete goals
- keep a record of prospects
- have honest and warm support
- engage in self-study
- feel that they belong to a successful group.

Achievement Motivation

The need to achieve is the spring board of the achievement motive. In a competitive society or set-up, the desire to excel over others or achieve a higher level than one's peers intensifies which in turn may lead to a stronger drive or motive to achieve something or everything that is essential to beat others in the race and consequently experience a sense of pride and pleasure in the achievement. The type of motivation produced by such desire for achievement is called the achievement motivation and has been defined in various ways.

Atkinson and Feather state that "the achievement motive is conceived as a latent disposition which is manifested in overt striving only when the individual perceives performance as instrumental to a sense of personal accomplishment".

Irving Sarnoff opines that "Achievement motive is defined in terms of the way an individual orients himself towards objects or conditions that he does not possess. If he values those objects and conditions and he feels that he ought to possess them he may regard as having an achievement motive".

McClelland and Atkinson note that "Achievement motivation may be associated with a variety of goals, but in general the behaviour adopted will involve activity which is directed towards the attainment of some standard of excellence. Competition with others in which they are beaten may be included in it."

From the above definitions, the achievement motivation moves or drives an individual to strive to gain mastery of difficult and challenging situations or performances in the pursuit of excellence. It comes into the picture when an individual knows that his performance will be evaluated, that the consequence of his actions will lead either to success or failure and that good performance will produce a feeling of pride in accomplishment. The achievement motive may thus be considered to be a disposition to approach success or the capacity to take pride in accomplishment when success is achieved in an activity.

The 'Theory of Achievement Motivation' was developed by MeClelland and his associates in 1951 at the University of Harward. According to him, human beings differ from one another in the strength of achievement motive. It is this difference is the strength of motivation to achieve that is important in understanding the differences in the economic growth of nations.

Development of achievement motivation is affected by a number of variables in home, school and society.

Home plays an important role in the early training of children for the development of attitudes and motives. Parental expectation and guidance to the child develop need for high achievement in life.

The society and its social philosophy is an important variable in developing achievement motivation. There are communities which are achievement-oriented. There are other societies which believe in fate and leave everything to God.

The child normally, now-a-days, enters the school at and age of 4 years. Before coming to school, the child gathers many experiences, which become an integral part of his personality and form his attitude towards life, but even then the school can help a lot to sharpen already acquired experiences and develop positive attitudes in children.

The teacher can play a very crucial role in the development of achievement motivation by these methods:

- The teacher should make clear the importance of achievement motive in life by means of telling the stories of great men and their achievements from all walks of life. When the students are convinced in advance to believe that they would or should develop achievement motive, the efforts of the teacher will succeed;
- The teacher should provide proper environment in the class and also outside the class. The teacher's attitude and enthusiasm will create better environment for achievement motive in children;
- The teacher will succeed in his attempt if he convinces the students that developing a new motive is realistic and reasonable;
- The teacher should relate the motive with future life of the students and assign independent responsibility to them;
- The teacher should make clear to the students that the new motive will improve their self-image;
- The teacher should emphasize upon the fact that new motive is an improvement on prevailing cultural values;
- The teacher should make students committed to achieving concrete goals in life related to the newly developed motive;
- The teacher should ask the students to keep the record of their progress towards their goal;
- The teacher should emphasize self-study;

- The teacher should make an effort to develop conducive social climate in the class that every individual should feel that he belongs to a group.

Achievement motivation is the expectancy of finding satisfaction in mastering challenging and difficult performances. It is the motivation to perform specific tasks for which there is a standard of excellence against which results can be judged. Hence, it should be at higher levels in students.

Evaluation in English

C.E. Beeby (1977) described the evaluation as "the systematic collection and interpretation of evidence leading, as part of the process, to a judgment of value with a view to action". There are four key elements in this definition. *First*, the use of the term 'systematic' implies that what information is needed will be defined with some degree of precision and that efforts to secure such information will be planned. The *second* element, 'interpretation of evidence' introduces critical consideration, sometimes over looked in evaluation. The *third* element, 'judgment of value' takes evaluation far beyond the level of mere description of what is happening in an educational enterprise. The *fourth* element 'with a view to action' introduces the distinction between an undertaking that results in a judgment of value with no specific reference to action and one that is deliberately undertaken for the sake of future action.

Evaluation is the heart of the educational process and it helps to determine whether the goal of schooling and the expected and desired behaviour changes have been attained or not. Progress in learning can be recognized by observation but such casual observation is incomplete and inaccurate and may be erroneous. Evaluation must be done systematically, and students' performance, their status, growth and development in various areas of behaviour and personality must be correctly, comprehensively and methodically appraised.

The effectiveness of instruction is usually determined by measuring achievements against objectives undertaken. An efficient programme of evaluation no longer comprise merely the effort to check the completed process but rather in the continual appraisal of the student's progress towards the attainment of pre-established aims. There is probably no more accurate barometer of the fundamental philosophy of any curriculum than a careful analysis of its evaluation programme.

The main purposes of the evaluation programme may be listed as:

- To help provide more intelligent guidance in teaching and learning;
- To develop more effective curricula and educative experiences;
- To secure more intelligent and effective co-operation from parents and community; and
- To provide an adequate and objective basis for reporting progress.

Apparently, when most persons think of evaluation they think of tests. Some one hundred million standardized tests of the true false, completion, matching or multiple choice type are used each year and many billions of pupils are tested each year by locally constructed objective and essay type examinations. If the numerous objectives set by the schools are to be evaluated, however, teachers must use many procedures for evaluation other than tests.

Among the lists of most common objectives set by school, one commonly finds such general headings as these:

- The development of effective ways of thinking;
- The cultivation of useful work habits and study skills;
- The inculcation of constructive social attitudes;
- The acquisition of a wide range of interests;

- The development of increased appreciation of music, art, literature and other aesthetic experiences;
- The development of social sensitivity;
- The development of better personal and social adjustment;
- The development of skill in reading, writing, oral and aural phases of language;
- The acquisition of important information;
- The development of physical health; and
- The development of consistent philosophy of life.

Evaluation of pupil's progress towards such objectives, with all their sub divisions, is not possible by means of tests. Evaluation is a much broader and more complex process than the giving of tests.

For evaluating pupil's work, one needs definite measures. Accuracy in the measurement of school products should be used to improve the learning of children and organization of the school and to find out those students who need remedial teaching, especially tutoring or transfer to other work. Examinations, as they are functioning, still dominate all levels of education. In teaching, evaluation is inevitable. It is this method that enables the teachers to know about the achievement of the students. Today, one of the aims of education is to bring about behavioural changes in the students in accordance with the objectives of the education or teaching. These are the standards that serve as measures of evaluation or achievement.

In English subject also, evaluation occupies an important place. The achievement of the students and their interest and the aptitude with regard to English can only be found out through the results of examinations. In fact, in the teaching of English, it is more required.

In India, the entire system of education is examination geared. The main purpose of the teaching is to enable the students to pass the examination. It has a sense of respectability attached to it. If a particular person passes a particular examination, he is considered competent and a person who fails to do is considered incompetent. The teaching of English has, therefore, also to keep in view the importance of the examination.

Generally, the tests or the methods of examinations are of three types:

1. Essay type examination (traditional type examination);
2. Short answer type tests; and
3. Objective type tests.

Essay type questions demand long answers. They allow relative freedom of response and make the students to recall than recognize.

An item covering 2 to 4 points is short answer type, and beyond this is essay type.

The objective type test items have only one fixed response or right answer. So, whoever corrects it any time, the score will be the same.

The objective type tests are of the following types:

1. Multiple choice items

   Example: Give answer with the correct word choosing from *a, b, c, d,* or *e.* "I am sorry. He's ... that he can't see you until Monday.

   (a) said

   (b) say

   (c) says

   (d) told

   (e) expressed

2. True or False items

   Example: State whether the following is true or false.

   Dolphins are found in aquariums. - T/F

3. Matching

Example: Match the words in column A with those of B.

A	B
(1) Robin	(a) Bright
(2) Hare	(b) Timid
(3) Lark	(c) Gentle
(4) Grass	(d) Little
(5) Windows	

4. Jumbled words

Write the letters in correct order.

- Lcohos
- Glenihs

5. Fill in the blanks. (With prepositions, conjunctions, articles, etc.)

Example: I bought this book ... ten rupees.

6. Completion

By the time he reached station, the train had already left. He was

7. One word answers

(a) Anil cut his finger.

(b) Ashish cut off his finger.

Q. Which boy has lost his finger?

8. Insert the missing letters:

(i) Te—c— — r

(ii) St—d—nt

In fact, it is true and premature to think of giving up the essay type of test or the traditional type of test. What is needed is the removal of the defects of the traditional type of tests, short answer type of tests and objective type of tests. This would make the examination system scientific. This is true with English as well.

With these aspects in mind, a study has been undertaken to study the level of achievement motivation and achievement in English and their relationship with each other at secondary school level.

Statement of the Problem

A Study of Achievement Motivation and Achievement in English of Secondary School Students

Need for the Study

Proper motivation of learning is one of the basic essentials of any set of educational experiences. The outcomes of such vital experiences are of different kinds, including certain knowledge, skills, abilities, understandings, attitudes, interests, appreciations and ways of living. Learning goes on the best in the degree that the individual sees and feels the significance to his own felt needs of what he does. Pupil's purpose is the prime move to the carrying out of learning experiences.

The vital role of motivation in life and learning is indisputable. Success and achievement in life and learning depend very largely on how much the student really want to succeed and achieve, what cost in human effort and energy the student is willing to bear to reach his goal, and what strong satisfactions he look forward to when he accomplishes his desire. In other words, the student's success and achievement in life and learning depends on his motivation. Motivation is the vital condition, the most powerful director of all learning. It is a factor in stimulating and directing learning. Teachers consider it as the art of stimulating and sustaining interest in learning.

Motivation is a process including the activities of an organism and determining its orientation. Motivation is the force that energizes and gives direction to behaviour and that underlies the tendency to persist.

Motivation can be increased by increasing need-for-achievement. Motivation can be developed in stages in training programmes. Training in behaviour such as how to take moderate risks, how to develop self-confidence in one's own ability to solve long range problems, how to be challenged by moderately difficult tasks, how to look for feedback of one's long range performance, and how to refer gratifications would help to develop a high need-for-achievement.

McClelland's hypothesis is that the achievement motive is the mainspring of entrepreneurial activity fostering the economic development of a society. McClelland found that too much pressure or too much perceived pressure might result in low achievement motivation. Other variables, which are influential, are sex of the child, size of the family, and occupation of the parents; achievement motivation also depends upon culture. He further observed that high achievers had developed an expectation of mastering challenging and difficult performances.

Achievement motivation is the key factor in achieving success in any task one performs. Whatever one learns, motivation plays a dominant role in making to learn that thing. Motivation and learning are interdependent. If one wants to learn something, one should try to develop interest in that through motivation.

It is equally true for learning of English. Proper foundation in the knowledge and skill of the subject English laid at school depends upon the motivation of the individual. Achievement motivation in learning English may be aroused if teachers provide them opportunities of utilizing their mental powers and exposure to various walks of life.

English is considered as a necessary subject for all the learners. It, like any other language, demands practice and application in the daily life which is possible only when the students have achievement motivation in learning. It is educationally unsound to teach English if the students do not show any interest.

The achievement motivation may also influence their regular attention in the classes, their aspirations to achieve in terms of marks, their choice of friends based on their interest and so on. Achievement motivation in English depends on the learning of the student in the subject.

If the students possess greater achievement motivation, they may be initiative, and confident to learn English in the class and from other English language and literature books, and to satisfy their deep and extensive interest. They may go on to satisfying their intellectual hunger. It can be a leisure time activity also.

Among the numerous reasons for poor performance in English, one of the reasons might be low motivation in the subject. Previous studies revealed that pupils having high motivation seem to achieve high scores in the subject. The level of achievement motivation of a student in the subject is responsible for the student's achievement in that particular subject. Ahluwalia (1985) proved that academic performance was positively and significantly related with achievement motivation. Mansuri (1986) found that the students having good general ability also had a high level of achievement motivation.

As a teacher of English, the investigator wanted to study the levels of achievement motivation and achievement in English of secondary school students and the relationship between achievement motivation and achievement in English.

Keeping all these in view, the investigator wanted to find out the answers to the following questions.

1. What are the different levels of achievement motivation?
2. What are the different levels of achievement in English?
3. Is there any difference in the level of achievement motivation between the sub-samples of identified variables?

4. Is there any difference in the level of achievement in English between the sub-samples of selected variables?
5. What is the relationship between achievement motivation and achievement in English?
6. Is there any difference in the level of relationship between achievement motivation and achievement in English in the sub-samples of selected variables?

Scope of the Study

The study was limited to identify the level of achievement motivation and achievement in English and their relationship of secondary school X class students of Guntur District.

The variables chosen for the study were gender of the student, management of the school, locality of the school and caste of the student. The sample size was limited to 284 selected from the secondary schools.

Objectives of the Study

The following were the objectives of the study:

1. To find out the level of achievement motivation of secondary school students;
2. To find out the difference in the achievement motivation between boy and girl students, rural and urban school students, private and government school students and reserved caste and unreserved caste students of secondary schools;
3. To find out the level of achievement in English of secondary school students;
4. To find out the difference in the achievement in English between boy and girl students, rural and urban school students, private and government school students, and reserved caste and unreserved caste students of secondary schools;

5. To find out the relationship between achievement motivation and achievement in English of secondary school students;
6. To find out the correlation between achievement motivation and achievement in English of boy and girl students, rural and urban school students, private and government school students, and reserved caste and unreserved caste students of secondary schools.

2 Review of Related Literature

"If we fail to build the foundation of knowledge provided by the review of literature, our work is likely to be shallow and will often be a duplicate work that has already been done by some one else". —*W.R. Borg*

Any worthwhile research study in any field of knowledge requires an adequate familiarity with the work which has already been done in the same area. A summary of the writings of recognised authorities and of previous research provides evidence that the research is familiar with what is already known and what is still unknown and untested. Since effective research is based upon past knowledge, this step helps to eliminate the duplication of what has been done and provides useful hypotheses and helpful suggestions for significant investigation.

Citing studies that show substantial agreement and those that seem to present conflicting conclusions help to sharpen and define understanding of existing knowledge in the problem area, provide a background for the research project and make the reader aware of the status of the issue. Parading a long list of annotated studies related to the problem is ineffective and inappropriate. Only those studies that are plainly relevant, competently executed and clearly reported should be included.

Capitalising on the reviews of expert researchers can be fruitful in providing helpful ideas and suggestions. While review articles that summarise related studies are useful, they do not provide a satisfactory substitute for an independent research. Even though the review of related literature is not a substitute for an independent work, it is one of the first steps in the research process. It is a valuable guide to define the problem, to recognise its significance, to suggest promising data-gathering devices, to appropriate study design and sources of data for effective analysis and to arrive at fruitful conclusions.

The need and importance of related studies and literature have been highlighted by Best as, "Particularly all human knowledge can be found is books and libraries. Unlike other animals that most start a new with each generation, man builds upon the accumulated and recorded knowledge of the past".

John Dewey has outlined the review of related studies as one of the important steps of scientific method. It is a crucial step, that invariably minimises the risk of dead ends, rejected topics, rejected studies, wasted efforts, trail and error activity extended towards approaches already discarded by previous investigations, and even more important erroneous findings based on the faulty research design.

Though the search for related literature is a time consuming process, it is necessary for a good research. Hence, this review.

ACHIEVEMENT MOTIVATION

The following were some of the related research studies on achievement motivation.

Achievement Motivation and Gender

- Baskaran, K. (1991) stated that there was no difference between achievement motivation of boys and girls.

- Gandhi, P. (1982) found no significant sex difference with respect to achievement motivation.
- Nagalakshmi, B. (1982) found that boys and girls did not differ significantly in achievement motivation.
- Gupta (1978) found that the sex difference did not play any role in achievement motivation.
- Ahluwalia (1985) stated that the sex of the child had no effect on achievement motivation.
- Chauhan (1984) stated that boys and girls did not differ significantly in relation to their achievement motivation.
- Raghava found that the boys and girls were possessing achievement motivation without any significant difference between them.
- Bharathi (1984) stated that there was no difference between achievement motivation of boys and girls.
- Jain (1983) found that there exists no significant sex difference in the concept of formation ability of four extreme groups, namely high intelligence — high achievement motivation group, high intelligence — low achievement motivation group, low intelligence — high achievement motivation group and low intelligence — low achievement motivation group.
- Lalitha (1982) found that the boys and girls were possessing achievement motivation without any significant difference between them.
- Gandhi (1982) stated that there was no significant sex difference with respect to achievement motive.
- Saraswat, Anil (1988) stated that boys and girls were significantly differed in their achievement motivation.
- Hari Krishna (1992) found that girls obtained a higher mean in achievement motivation than boys.
- Gandhi, P. (1982) reported that high school girls had significantly higher motive than high school boys.

- Gokulnathan (1971), and Gokulnathan and Mehta (1972) reported higher need for achievement in girls than higher need for achievement in boys.
- Gawande, E.N. (1988) had found that boys and girls were significantly differed in their achievement motivation, boys were more achievement motivated than girls.
- Sinha, J.K.P. (1986) stated that boys had higher achievement motivation than girls.
- Abrol (1977) noticed that boys tend to have higher achievement motivation than girls.

Achievement Motivation and Locality of the School

- Ahluwalia (1985) found that urban/rural up-bringing had no effect on achievement motivation of children.
- Bhaskaran (1991) observed that urban and rural students did not differ in the level of achievement motivation.
- Saraswat, Anil (1988) stated that rural and urban students were significantly differed in their achievement motivation.
- Sharma, R. (1985) found a significant difference in the achievement motivation of rural and urban students.
- Gawande, E.N. (1988) stated that achievement of urban students was at higher level than that of rural students.

Achievement Motivation and School Management

- Ahluwalia, I. (1985) found that government and private schools did not significantly affect the achievement motivation of children.
- Baskaran, K. (1991) noticed that government school and aided private school students did not differ significantly in achievement motivation.

Achievement Motivation and Grades

- Mansuri (1986) in a study with the students of V, VI and VII grades found that grade was an effective variable in achievement motivation. The students of successive grades had successive advancement in achievement motivation.

Achievement Motivation and School Subjects

- Chatterji, P. S. reported that the scores of achievement motivation of students of science or commerce were significantly higher than those of other groups.

Achievement Motivation and Caste

- Dutt (1983) found that the tribal students with high achievement motivation were better than students having low achievement motivation with regard to intelligence and extra version.

Achievement Motivation and Intelligence

- Jain (1983) found that the intelligence was found to a better predictor of concept formation ability than achievement motivation.
- Narula (1979) studied achievement motivation in relation to intelligence, SES and performance of secondary school teachers in Orissa and reported that these were independent of need for achievement (n-ach).

Achievement Motivation and Stress

- Gupta (1979) reported a positive relationship between psychological stress and achievement motivation.

Achievement Motivation and Prejudices

- Sinha (1986) found that prejudices influenced the achievement motivation in a negative way and high prejudiced males and females had higher achievement motivation.

ACHIEVEMENT IN ENGLISH

Some of the research studies related to achievement in English were quoted below:

Achievement in English and Gender

- Raghawan, R. found that males were found to have significantly higher academic achievement than females.
- Baskaran, K. (1991) found a significant difference between boys and girls in their achievement; girls scored higher than boys.
- Hari Krishnan, M. (1992) found a significant difference in the mean scores of boys and girls of their achievement.
- Rani, Radha (1992) reported that sex difference existed in academic achievement.
- Mazumdar, Angira (1992) stated that there was no significant differences between boys and girls in respect of their achievement and attitude scores.
- Singh, Manju (1989) stated that the difference in the mean scores of boys and girls in achievement in English was found to be insignificant.

Achievement in English and Locality

- Singh, R.D. (1983) found that rural students received lower marks than the urban students.
- Baskaran, K. (1991) stated that urban and rural students differed significantly in their achievement.
- Nagaraju, M.T.V., K. Sumalatha and V. Govinda (2003) found that the performance of urban students was significantly higher than that of rural students in academic achievement.
- Shahapur, N.P. (2004) found a significant difference was found between rural and urban Devadasi children in respect of their academic achievement.

- Singh, Manju (1989) stated that no significant differences between the mean scores of the rural and urban students.

Achievement in English and School Management

- Singh (1986) found that the difference in English achievement was significant for low and high groups in n-ach in case of Delhi schools, but in case of Haryana schools, it was not significant.
- Sharma (1981) noticed that poor academic motivation, poor linguistic ability, poor planning of study work, poor adjustment and emotional insecurity contributed to under achievement of rural girls in secondary schools of Haryana.
- De Sai, S.D. (1979) has reported that the level of classroom climate was positively related to pupils motivation and their academic achievement.

Achievement in English and School Subjects

- Saraswat, Anil (1988) reported that Science and Arts students significantly differed in their academic achievement, occupational aspiration and achievement motivation.

RELATIONSHIP BETWEEN ACHIEVEMENT IN ENGLISH AND ACHIEVEMENT MOTIVATION

Achievement Motivation and Achievement — Gender

- Chandy, Sumi (1991) reported that achievement motivation was significantly and positively related to academic achievement of high school students of both the sexes.
- Fatmi (1986) found that the sex influenced the achievement related motivations. Non-tribals, girls, Hindu and forward and backward caste groups were superior in achievement related motivations. The

achievement motivation of a person had significantly a positive correlation with other achievement related motivations.

- Gawande, E.N. (1988) stated that the correlation between achievement motivation and scholastic achievement of boys was more than girls.
- Gandhi, P. (1982) reported that achievement motivation was significantly and positively related to academic achievement of high school students of both sexes.
- Pandey, Kalpalata (1985) stated that except for the self-concept and achievement in Hindi, high deprived boys and girls did not differ significantly.
- Saraswat, Anil (1988) reported that boys and girls significantly differed in their academic achievement, occupational aspiration and achievement motivation.

Achievement Motivation and Achievement — Caste

- Rani (1980) found no significant relationship existed between academic achievement and achievement anxiety and perception of purpose in life for both SC and non-SC students.
- Gawande, E.N. (1988) stated that there was no significant difference in the coefficient of correlation of achievement motivation and scholastic achievement of non-backward and backward students.

Achievement Motivation and Achievement — Locality

- Saraswat, Anil (1988) stated that rural and urban students significantly differed in their academic achievement, occupational aspiration and achievement motivation.

Achievement Motivation and Achievement — School Subjects

- Singh (1986) found that correlations between n-ach and *(a)* intellectual efficiency; *(b)* introversion-extroversion;

(*c*) socio-cultural status; and (*d*) achievement were found significant.

- Khanna (1982) found that the n-ach was significant on all achievement related words. The main effect of n-ach was significant on achievement related statements.
- Pandey, Kalpalata (1985) reported that high deprived boys possessed a significant relationship between achievement in Social Studies and Hindi language.
- Devanesan, Paul P. (1990) stated that there was a significant positive relationship between achievement motivation and scholastic achievement of higher secondary students.
- Mazumdar, Angiea (1992) stated that the co-efficient of correlation between achievement in English and attitude towards English was positive.
- Saraswat, Anil (1988) found that the co-efficients of correlation among achievement motivation, occupational aspiration and academic achievement were significant.

Though, there were studies related to achievement motivation and achievement, they were not exactly the substitutes for the proposed study. Hence, now, a study on achievement motivation and achievement in English of secondary school students has been undertaken.

3 Research Methodology

Research is a systematic enquiry seeking facts through objective and verifiable methods in order to discover the relationship among them and to deduce from the broad principles or laws. Therefore, the very success of a research work depends upon collecting the necessary information. Several methods of collecting information are developed to assist the research. Every survey expert has his own ideas of selecting the best method of collecting information. But, it cannot be uniform to all. The selection of the method depends on the type of information to be gathered and the sources of information to be consulted. For the present study, normative survey method was chosen.

Survey intends the interpretation of things rigorously and comprehensively. Now-a-days, survey method is a popular way of collecing data for analysing the results statistically and systematically. This method is suitable to this study as this one is a status study.

OPERATIONAL DEFINITIONS OF THE KEY TERMS

The operational definitions of the important terms used in the present study were discussed and defined herewith:

Achievement Motivation

The basis of achievement motivation is achievement motive, that is, the motive to achieve. Those who engage themselves in a task on account of an achievement motive are said to work under the spirit of achievement motivation. The desire to improve his performance at school or to get a good grade or to become an engineer is known as achievement motive. The theory of achievement motivation was developed by McClelland and his associates in 1951 at the University of Harward. Achievement motive may be considered as a disposition to approach success or a capacity for taking pride in accomplishment when success at one or another activity is achieved. Achievement motivation is an expectancy of finding satisfactions in mastery of difficult and challenging performances. In the field of education, it stands for the pursuit of excellence. The person, who is more motivated to achieve, tries to maximize his own anxiety about failure, struggles hard for getting success and derives maximum pleasure from success.

Achievement Motivation Scale

Various attempts have been made to design some measures for the measurement of achievement motivation. The investigator has taken for use the Achievement Motivation Scale standardized by Dr. Shah Beena. There are 40 partly completed sentences in this test. Each sentence can be completed meaningfully if one links it up with any one of the alternatives offered. The task is to select only one answer which seems to correspond most with one's present feelings and then put a tick mark (✓) against the selected alternative. All the items in the test have to be answered.

Achievement in English

The subject English plays an important role in the school curriculum to develop language and communicative skills in pupils, which will in turn enable them to become good citizens of the present cybernetic world. The assessment or the attainment in the subject is also very important to sort the students into different categories and to encourage them to study the subject effectively and to field remedial measures for all types of problems in the subject.

Achievement Test in English

Freeman defines a test of educational achievement as a test designed to measure knowledge, understanding, skills in a specified subject or group of subjects. Thus, an educational achievement test measures an individual's knowledge, understanding or skills in a particular branch of knowledge. The standardized achievement tests are used to determine the degree of achievement in a specific subject matter. Achievement test attempts to measure what an individual has learned and to assess his or her present level of performance. It is also used for the purposes of guidance and counselling. It is also useful in remedial teaching programmes as well as in determining the class to which a student should be admitted into. Frequently, achievement test scores are used in evaluating the influence of courses of study, teachers, teaching methods and other factors considered to be significant in educational practice. The achievement in English measures the performance of the students in English in an examination. For the present study, the marks secured in English by the X class students in the public examinations conducted by the government of Andhra Pradesh.

Secondary School

A school that runs classes from 8th to 10th is a secondary school.

Rural School

A school located in rural areas is a rural school.

Urban School

A school located in urban areas is an urban school.

Government School

A school run by Government, Zilla Parishad or Municipality is a government school.

Private School

A school managed by private individuals or organizations is a private school.

Reserved Castes

The castes that are included in SC, ST and BC categories by the Government of Andhra Pradesh are referred to as reserved castes.

Unreserved Castes

The castes that were excluded from the reservation categories are unreserved castes.

VARIABLES OF THE STUDY

A variable, as the name implies, is something that varies. This is the simplest and broadest way of defining a variable. However, a behaviour scientist defines the variables as those attributes of objects, events, things, and beings that can be measured. In other words, variables are those characters or conditions that are manipulated, controlled or observed by the investigator. The variables are the necessary requisites for any worthwhile research for the purpose of comparison.

The variables considered for the present study were:

- Boys *versus* Girls of Secondary Schools
- Rural *versus* Urban Secondary School Students
- Private *versus* Government Secondary School Students
- Reserved Caste *versus* Unreserved Caste Students of Secondary Schools

The rationale for choosing the above stated variables was discussed herewith:

Boys *versus* Girls

Sex was taken as a variable to see if there was any significant difference between boys and girls in possessing achievement motivation and achievement in English.

In olden days, the boys were educated and the girls were restricted to their kitchens by their adult community; times changed and the adults recognized the importance of women education. In the words of late Prime Minister Jawaharlal Nehru, "If you educate a man, you educate only one person. If you educate a woman, you educate the entire family." In the due course of time, women's education gained importance and many parents are encouraging their daughters to pursue higher education and even allowing them to go abroad. The women are also showing excellence in all fields. Their presence is felt almost in all fields.

As the physiological condition, exposure to society, education and other aspects of girls and boys vary differently; there may be a significant difference in the possession of achievement motivation and achievement in English. The boys may be exposed to the society to a larger extent, but the girls spend most of their time either in going through books or helping their parents at home. These factors will show their influence on achievement motivation and achievement in English.

It is also especially important to study the level of possession of achievement motivation and achievement in English of secondary school students because they just enter the adolescent stage, which is otherwise known as the period of stress and strain. At this stage, the sample finds it extremely difficult to adjust themselves in the society because they are accepted neither as adults nor as children. It is also familiar that girls mature faster than boys at the early adolescent stage, both physically and mentally. The above factors will also have their impact on the possession of achievement motivation and achievement in English.

So, a comparison between boys and girls will reveal of any difference that exists in the possession of achievement motivation and achievement in English.

Rural *versus* Urban Secondary School Students

Generally, the urban schools are well equipped in many aspects when compared to rural schools. The buildings, the libraries, the laboratories, the teaching staff, the educational atmosphere, the competitive spirit among the pupils, the amenities provided to pupils to pursue education, the exposure to fairs and exhibitions, the student participation in teaching, the learning process, the use of audio-visual teaching aids, etc., will always be better in urban schools than in rural schools. Even if the rural and urban secondary schools have equal level of amenities, facilities, and other benefits, the attitude of teachers and students will have their own impact on motivation and achievement.

A comparison between rural and urban school students will bring out the difference in the level of possession of achievement motivation and achievement in English.

Private *versus* Government Secondary School Students

The reputation of private schools is generally better when compared to the government schools. In private schools, the pupils are exposed to better conditions and better study atmosphere. The school laboratory, library facilities, etc., will be better in private schools. If better facilities are not provided in private schools, the parents will question the authorities concerned, because they pay higher fees for the education of their children. The quality of teaching is also supposed to be better in private schools. The teachers take more interest in teaching in private schools as they are always either in the fear of losing their jobs or immediately being questioned by the managements about the quality of their teaching.

Thus, it is important to assess the level of achievement motivation and achievement in English of private and government school students for comparison.

Reserved *versus* Unreserved Caste Students of Secondary Schools

The Education Commission (1964-66) stressed the need for providing equal educational opportunities to all sections of the populations belonging to different regions, castes and religions. Equalization of educational opportunity means providing suitable education for all in accordance with their interest, abilities and attitudes. The modern trend in the social change is towards the establishment of equality, freedom, justice and fraternity in the social order. The term reserved caste is used mainly in the context of Indian society.

The problems of the children from the reserved communities are interwoven, each being a cause and effect of the other. For example, when the occupation of the family is menial it does not fetch adequate wages and low wages lead to poverty. This poverty often becomes the cause of ill health, malnutrition, inferior surroundings or habits. Parents of these children were also born in these conditions. They did not have access to schooling and education. The children of such families have to earn their livings from very young age. Naturally, they cannot go to school and so they remain illiterate. Thus, the awareness that comes with formal schooling and the job opportunities available for literates are denied to them and in return to their children. Some children have to work for longer hours at their houses and they cannot go to schools. Many children live in villages and hence they do not have convenient schools.

Under these circumstances, it was decided to compare the levels of achievement motivation and achievement in English of reserved and unreserved caste students.

HYPOTHESES OF THE STUDY

The hypothesis is a tentative answer to a question. It is a hunch or an educated guess, to be subjected to the process of verification or confirmation. Hypotheses are suggested problem solutions, which are expressed as generalizations or prepositions. They are the statements consisting of elements expressed in an orderly system of relationships which seek to describe or to explain events that have not yet been confirmed by facts. They may provide the conceptual elements that complete the known data, conceptual relationships that systematize unordered elements or conceptual meanings and interpretations that explain the unknown phenomena. By logically relating known facts and intelligent guesses about unknown conditions can be made, the hypotheses are able to extend and enlarge our knowledge.

John W. Best identifies four basic characteristics of a good hypothesis: it should be reasonable, it should be consistent with known facts or theories, it should be stated in such a way that it can be tested and found to be probably true or probably false, and it should be stated in the simplest possible terms.

With these criteria as a frame of reference, the following working hypotheses were formulated for the present study.

The three major hypotheses and their rationale have been discussed. Each one of the main hypothesis has been studied in further detail by forming sub-hypotheses under each head.

Hypothesis 1

"The secondary school students are possessing high achievement motivation".

Motivation is one of the most important conditions of learning. A high degree of motivation helps in arousing students into action and ensuring active participation in learning activities. The teacher has to direct the learning process and must be aware of the nature of important motives. Development of achievement motive is affected by a number of variables in home, school and society. Home plays an important role in the early training of children for the development of attitudes and motives. Parental expectation and guidance to the child develop need for achievement in life. The society and its social philosophy is an important variable in developing achievement motive. There are communities which are achievement-oriented.

Before coming to school, the child gathers many experiences, which become an integral part of his personality and form his attitude towards life. But even then, the school helps a lot to sharpen already acquired experiences and develops positive attitudes in children. The teacher can play a very crucial role in the development of achievement motive by following these methods:

- The teacher should make clear the importance of achievement motive in life by means of telling the stories of great men and their achievements from all walks of life. When the students are convinced in advance to believe that they would or should develop achievement motive, the efforts of the teacher will succeed;
- The teacher should provide proper environment in the classes and outside the class. The teacher's attitude and enthusiasm will create better environment for the development of achievement motive in children;
- The teacher will succeed in his attempt if he convinces the students that developing a new motive is realistic and reasonable;
- The teacher should relate the motive with future life of the students and assign independent responsibility to them;
- The teacher should make clear to the students that the new motive will improve their self image;
- The teacher should emphasize upon the fact that new motive is an improvement on prevailing cultural values;
- The teacher should make students committed in achieving concrete goals in life related to the newly developed motive;

- ❖ The teacher should ask the students to keep the record of their progress towards their goal;
- ❖ Self study should be emphasized;
- ❖ The teacher should make an effort to develop conducive social climate in the class so that every individual should feel that he belongs to a group.

As stated earlier, under the area of achievement motivation, the variables, namely, boys versus girls, rural versus urban, government versus private, and reserved versus unreserved caste students were considered. To study each of these variables in detail, the following sub-hypotheses were formulated:

Hypothesis 1A

"There is a significant difference in the achievement motivation of boy and girl secondary school students".

Hypothesis 1B

"There is a significant difference in the of achievement motivation of rural and urban secondary school students".

Hypothesis 1C

"There is a significant difference in the achievement motivation of private and government secondary school students".

Hypothesis 1D

"There is a significant difference in the achievement motivation of reserved and unreserved caste secondary school students".

Hypothesis 2

"The secondary school students are possessing high achievement in English".

Achievement is of a paramount importance, particularly in the present socio-economic and cultural contexts, and hence great emphasis is placed on achievement right from the beginning of the formal education. It is a task-oriented behaviour that allows the individuals' performance to be evaluated according to some internally or externally imposed criterion that involves some standard of excellence.

Achievement is related to the acquisition of principles and generalizations and the capacity to perform efficiently certain manipulations of objects, symbols and ideas. Assessment of achievement has been largely confirmed to the evaluation in terms of knowledge and understanding. It is universally accepted that the acquisition of factual data is not an end in itself but that an individual who has received education should show the evidence of having understood them. But, for obvious reasons, the examinations are largely confined to the measurement of the amount of information acquired by the students.

Achievement in terms of subject matter is conventionally assured in one institution by employing a system of marks or grades and it has been strongly argued that marks are necessary for effective teaching and learning. Marks also set goals and motivate students. It is universally accepted that marks serve as the basis of classification and certification.

Under the achievement in English, the following three sub-hypotheses were framed.

Hypothesis 2A

"There is a significant difference in the achievement in English of boy and girl secondary school students".

Hypothesis 2B

"There is a significant difference in the achievement in English of rural and urban secondary school students".

Hypothesis 2C

"There is a significant difference in the achievement in English of private and government secondary school students".

Hypothesis 2D

"There is a significant difference in the achievement in English of reserved and unreserved caste secondary school students".

Hypothesis 3

"There is a positive correlation between achievement motivation and achievement in English of secondary school students".

Many studies indicate a relationship between achievement motivation and academic achievement. Suitable suggestions may be placed before the teachers and planners if there is a relationship between these two for helping students in achieving excellence in their academic endeavors.

Under the area of relationship between achievement motivation and achievement in English of secondary school students, the following three sub-hypotheses were framed.

Hypothesis 3A

"There is a positive correlation between achievement motivation and achievement in English of boy and girl secondary school students".

Hypothesis 3B

"There is a positive correlation between achievement motivation and achievement in English of rural and urban secondary school students".

Hypothesis 3C

"There is a positive correlation between achievement motivation and achievement in English of private and government secondary school students".

Hypothesis 3D

"There is a positive correlation between achievement motivation and achievement in English of reserved and unreserved caste secondary school students".

SAMPLE OF THE STUDY

A population is any group of individuals that has one or more characteristics in common. The populations may be all the individuals of a particular type or a more restricted part of that group.

A sample is a small proportion of a population selected for observations and analysis. By observing the characteristics of the sample, one can make certain influences about the characteristics of the population from which it is drawn.

The students studying tenth class in the secondary schools will be the population of the study. Out of the total population, a representative sample of 284 students will be selected for the present study using stratified random sampling technique. Details of sample selection are given hereunder.

After finalizing the variables of the present study, consideration was given to whether the entire population is to be made the subject for data collection or a particular group is to be selected as representative of the whole population. Here, population refers to all the tenth class students of the secondary schools of Andhra Pradesh. Of the two techniques, the second one, namely, the selection of a group as a representative of the whole population was found to be more convenient and suitable. This technique leads to a considerable saving of time, effort and finance. The number of students selected is small, and so it is possible to make a detailed and intensive study. This generally leads to more accurate and reliable results. As this sampling technique has many advantages, it was selected for the collection of data. Sampling is simply the process of learning about the population on the basis of a sample drawn from it.

In any social research, various methods are utilized for selection and drawing of samples. After a detailed study of all these methods and considering the variables selected for the research work, the stratified sampling method was found to be most suitable.

In the stratified sampling method, the entire population will be divided into smaller homogeneous groups (Best) or strata, and then the sample is selected within each group. Every sampling unit in the population is placed in one of the strata prior to the selection of the sample so that the sum of the strata is identical with the population.

Stratified sampling method has certain merits and advantages as a technique of sampling. Auckof has rightly said that stratified sampling enables the researcher to make a comparison of properties or traits as well as to estimate population characteristics (Kerlinger, 1964).

In stratified sampling method, the investigator has greater control over the selection of the sample when compared with random sampling. In random sampling, although every group has a chance of being selected and included in the sample, there is every possibility and sometimes it does happen that certain important groups are left unrepresented. But, in stratified sampling method, no important group is likely to be left out.

Stratified sampling method is the ideal one when comparison between different variables has to be made. For example, if comparison has to be made between boys and girls or rural and urban pupils, it would be very difficult to select the required number of units through any other method of sampling. If any other method is used, the problem of bias and prejudice creeps in.

Replacement of units is also possible in the stratified sampling method. Normally, if a particular unit is not accessible for a study, it is difficult to replace it by another, but in this method it is possible. Stephens states that stratification automatically brings about a replacement of persons lost to the sample by persons of the same stratum, thus partly correcting the bias that would result if there were no replacement of losses. As the entire population is divided into particular strata, it is easy and convenient to replace an inaccessible one by an accessible one.

In stratified sampling method, much depends on the stratification process. The following precautions were taken while stratifying the population: the variables involved in the study were taken note of, care was taken to see that each stratum in the universe was large enough in size so that selection of items could be done on random basis, the strata formed were definite and clear and each stratum was free from the influence of others, and that there was no overlapping.

Before actually selecting the sample, certain fundamental principles were considered to make the sample scientific and clear-cut.

Firstly, the 'Universe' was clearly defined. In the technical phraseology of research, the whole population out of which the samples are selected is known as the 'Universe'. For the present research work, the universe includes all the students of tenth class studying in secondary schools of Andhra Pradesh. The study was limited to a particular geographical area, i.e., Guntur district, to facilitate appropriate sample selection.

Secondly, a decision has to be made about the units of the sample as the unit of a sample may be a house, a family, a group of individuals or a single individual. A good unit should possess the following characteristics.

(*A*) **Clarity:** The unit should be clearly defined in unambiguous terms. This would make the study easy and efficient. For the present research work, a sampling unit was defined as a student of tenth class studying in any secondary school of Andhra Pradesh.

(*B*) **Suitability:** A good unit should be well suited to the problem under study. Since the problem is the possession and comparison of achievement motivation and achievement in English of the tenth class students of secondary schools of Andhra Pradesh, the unit selected is well suited to the problem.

(C) **Accessibility:** The unit selected should be easily accessible to the researcher. If the units selected are difficult to reach and if he fails to make use of them, the study would be vitiated. The selected sampling unit, i.e., a tenth class student is easily accessible since he/ she could be approached in any secondary school.

Besides considering these principles, it is extremely important to think about the size of the sample to be selected. If the sample is either too small or too large, it will make the study difficult and also make the results untenable. An optimum sample in survey is one which fulfils the requirements of effective representativeness, reliability and flexibility. The sample should be small enough to avoid intolerable sampling error. The size of sample for the present research work was decided after considering the following factors.

Since an intensive study was planned, a very large number of samples were not selected. In case of an intensive study, very large numbers of samples are not so useful as they involve huge consumption of resources. A smaller sample is very much convenient.

The size and selection of the samples will also be influenced by the nature of the universe. If the universe is homogenous, even a small-sized sample may yield dependable and required results. If the universe is heterogeneous, small-sized samples may not be useful. In case of the present study, the heterogeneous universe will be split into smaller homogenous groups and the samples will be selected from these strata. For example, all the tenth class students will be broadly grouped under boys and girls. Required sample will be selected from each of these two groups.

The investigator needs to determine the number of groups to be formed. In case the number of groups proposed is large, the size of the samples shall have to be large so that every group should be of proper in size and suit to the requirements of the study. In case the number of groups proposed is small, even small-sized samples can fulfill the requirement. In case of the present study, the number of groups into which the universe was divided are girls and boys, rural and urban students, government and private school students, and reserved and unreserved caste students. Since the number of groups is moderate, a reasonably large sample was selected from each of these groups.

Practical considerations and accuracy will also play a vital role in determining the size of the sample. Every study is guided by certain practical considerations such as time, resources, accessibility of data, etc. Generally, it is believed that a large-sized sample is more representative and generally produces accurate results. This, of course, depends upon the technique of sampling used. If the technique is scientific, even small-sized samples can produce dependable and accurate results. While selecting the size of the sample for the present study, practical considerations like the availability of resources and time were taken into consideration. Care was taken to make the sample selection technique as scientific as possible.

The size of the sample is also governed by the size of the tools to be used. In case the tools are short and the questions asked pertain to certain limited factors, a large sample can be selected. In case the tools are large and the questions complicated, the sample should be small in size so that, from administrative point of view, the investigator may not be put to unnecessary troubles. In the present study, the tool was quite elaborate; hence a very large sample was not selected.

The sampling method also determines the size of the sample. When random sampling method is used, the samples have to be large. On the other hand, if samples are selected through stratified sampling method, the reliability can be achieved even with the help of the small-sized samples.

After taking into consideration all these factors, which influence the size of the sample, it was decided that an ideal sample would consist of 284 tenth class students. This sample is small enough to avoid unnecessary expenditure and large enough to avoid intolerable sampling errors.

After deciding about the sampling method and the size of the sample, the universe selected was divided into different strata. The variables chosen for the study were considered to divide the universe. The sample consists of boys — 140, girls — 140, rural students — 143, urban students — 141, government school students — 200, private school students — 84, reserved caste students — 163, unreserved caste students — 121.

TOOLS OF THE STUDY

A research tool plays a major role in any worthwhile research as it is the sole factor in determining the sound data and in arriving at perfect conclusions about the problem or study in hand, which, ultimately, helps in providing suitable remedial measures to the problem concerned.

A great variety of research tools has been developed to aid in the acquisition of data. These tools are of many kinds and employ distinctive ways of describing and quantifying data. Each tool is particularly appropriate for certain sources of data, yielding information of the kind and in the form that would be most effectively used, like the tools in the carpenter's chest, each is appropriate in a given situation.

The selection and use of tools can be done in two ways:

The *first* one is to construct a tool independently by the investigator for his/her own study. Here, there are many problems in doing so. Preparation and standardization of a perfect tool itself is a major task, and one can easily say that it is a doctoral study itself. On construction of their own tools, Anand and Padma (1987) felt that "A note of caution has to be struck when a researcher develops a tool for his study by merely pooling up some items and does not subject it to the sophisticated techniques of tool construction. The result would be then, obviously, a poor quality research". With this, one can say that preparation and standardization of tools is a major task, and one should take care in aspects like selection of area and sample, pooling up of statements related to the area and sample, consulting the experts, and application of sophisticated statistical techniques.

The *second* way of selection and use of tools is right selection of tools from already standardized ones available in the field of study. Here also it involves a tedious job in locating the tools and identifying their usefulness to the study on hand. Even then, this technique is very useful when a research work is taken to study in depth and when the research work involves a good number of variables. Some people believe that some of the instruments available do not measure up to their standards. Hence, new ones. In some instances, consideration should be given to the logistics of the situation. Lacking of time and financial resources, many researches cannot expect to produce a better instrument. In these cases, the most logical procedure that one can follow is to choose the best instrument available for his purpose.

Considering the flaws and merits of the selection of tools either way, the investigator was interested in using the standardized tools as the present study involves a thorough study of achievement motivation and achievement in English of secondary school students and their relationship with each other.

Measurement of Achievement Motivation

After a thorough survey of literature, the investigator identified the Achievement Motivation Scale (AMS) of Beena Shah was found to be useful.

The Achievement Motivation Scale Covers Need for Academic Success, Need for Vocational Achievement, Need for Social Achievement and Need for Skill Achievement.

Measurement of Achievement in English

To measure the achievement in English, marks of English obtained in public examination, which was conducted by the Government of Andhra Pradesh for all the students of the state were used. The reason for taking these marks is that the examination is common to every student of every secondary school in the state. And also, the achievement in English may be as per the ability of a student as the paper is common to every student in the state.

Both the tools were having relevancy to the study in collecting the data from the sample.

ADMINISTRATION OF THE TOOL

The Achievement Motivation Scale was administered personally and gathered the data from the sample. After this, the marks in English of each student were collected from the concerned school later after the public examination marks were received by the concerned school from the government.

4 Analysis of Data

Analysis of the data is the most skilled task of all stages of research. Analysis of data means studying the tabulated material in order to determine inherent facts of meanings. It involves breaking down complex factors into simple ones and putting the parts in new arrangements for the purpose of interpretation.

The first step in the analysis of data is a critical examination of the assembled data. This includes coding, editing and tabulation. Coding involves assigning symbols to each response, the purpose of which is to translate raw data into symbols and this depends on proper coding of responses. Editing can be helpful for coding and for improving the quality of data collection. Tabulation is a means of recording classification in a compact form in such a way so as to facilitate comparisons.

The method of analysis chosen for a particular study depends upon the mature of objectives, hypotheses to be tested, and the purpose and use of the study. Statistical methods are the mathematical techniques used to facilitate the interpretation of numerical data secured from groups of individuals or group of observations or a single individual.

In the present study, "A Study of Achievement Motivation and Achievement in English of Secondary School Students", several statistical techniques were used to perform the analysis. After collecting the data from the two hundred and eighty four secondary school tenth class students, the analysis was performed keeping in view the objectives framed, hypotheses formulated. For this purpose, mean, standard deviation, critical ratio, Pearson correlation, etc., were employed.

Hypothesis 1

"The secondary school students are possessing high achievement motivation".

To test the validity of the above hypothesis, the mean and standard deviation were calculated. The results are as follows:

Table 4.1 Achievement Motivation of Secondary School Students

Sample	Mean	Standard Deviation
284	65.71	17.76

The students studying in secondary schools were holding high achievement motivation. As per the standard deviation, there was a high dispersion of scores in the units of sample.

The hypothesis that "the secondary school students are possessing high achievement motivation" can be accepted as there is a high achievement motivation in secondary school students.

Hypothesis 1A

"There is a significant difference in the achievement motivation of boy and girl secondary school students".

A comparison of the achievement motivation scores of boys and girls was made to find out the difference in the achievement motivation possessed by them. The data are as follows:

Table 4.2 Comparison of Achievement Motivation of Boy and Girl Students of Secondary Schools

Variable	Sample	Mean	S.D.	M.D.	C.R.
Boys	140	64.64	17.08	2.33	1.45*
Girls	144	66.97	8.48		

* Not significant at 0.05 level.

It can be observed, from Table 4.2, that the boys and girls of secondary schools were holding high achievement motivation without any significant difference between them.

The hypothesis that "there is a significant difference in the achievement motivation of boy and girl secondary school students" can be rejected as there is no significant difference in the achievement motivation of boys and girls of secondary schools.

Hypothesis 1B

"There is a significant difference in the achievement motivation of rural and urban secondary school students".

The following calculations were made to test the validity of the hypothesis.

Table 4.3 Comparison of Achievement Motivation of Rural and Urban Secondary School Students

Variable	Sample	Mean	S.D.	M.D.	C.R.
Rural	143	68.15	9.81	6.31	3.52*
Urban	141	61.84	17.58		

* Significant at 0.05 level.

As can be seen from Table 4.3, there was a significant difference in the achievement motivation possessed by rural and urban secondary school students. The rural students were holding higher achievement motivation than their counterparts. Both rural and urban secondary school students fall under high achievement motivation category.

The hypothesis that "there is a significant difference in the achievement motivation of rural and urban secondary school students" can be accepted as there is a significant difference in the achievement motivation of rural and urban secondary school students.

Hypothesis 1C

"There is a significant difference in the achievement motivation of private and government secondary school students".

The following calculations were made to test the validity of the hypothesis.

Table 4.4 Comparison of Achievement Motivation of the Private and Government Secondary School Students

Variable	Sample	Mean	S.D.	M.D.	C.R.
Government	200	64.35	21.12	21.9	3.22*
Private	84	66.25	8.22		

* Significant at 0.05 level.

Though both government and private secondary school students hold a high achievement motivation, the private school students were possessing significantly higher achievement motivation than government school students.

The hypothesis that "there is a significant difference in the achievement motivation of private and government secondary school students" can be accepted as there is a significant difference in the achievement motivation of private and government secondary school students.

Hypothesis 1D

"There is a significant difference in the achievement motivation of reserved and unreserved caste secondary school students".

The following calculations were made to test the validity of the hypothesis.

Table 4.5 Comparison of Achievement Motivation of Reserved and Unreserved Caste Secondary School Students

Variable	Sample	Mean	S.D.	M.D.	C.R.
Reserved	163	63.54	17.85	6.2	2.6*
Un-reserved	121	69.74	14.62		

* Significant at 0.05 level.

The reserved and unreserved caste students of secondary schools were holding high achievement motivation and the achievement motivation was significantly high in unreserved caste students than reserved caste students.

The hypothesis that "there is a significant difference in the achievement motivation of reserved and unreserved caste secondary school students" can be accepted as there is a significant difference in the achievement motivation of reserved and unreserved caste secondary school students.

Hypothesis 2

"The secondary school students are possessing high achievement in English".

To test the validity of the hypothesis, the following calculations were made and the results are as follows.

Table 4.6 Achievement in English of Secondary School Students

Sample	Mean	Standard Deviation
284	95.88	8.42

The students studying in secondary schools were holding high achievement in English. As per the standard deviation, there was a lower dispersion of scores in the units of sample.

The hypothesis that "the secondary school students are possessing high achievement in English" can be accepted as the secondary school students are possessing high achievement in English.

Hypothesis 2A

"There is a significant difference in the achievement in English of boy and girl of secondary school students".

The following calculations were made to test the validity of the hypothesis.

Table 4.7 Comparison of Achievement Motivation of Boy and Girl Secondary School Students

Variable	Sample	Mean	S.D.	M.D.	C.R.
Boys	140	95.27	8.36	1.19	1.3*
Girls	144	96.46	8.48		

* Not significant at 0.05 level.

From the mean scores of Table 4.6, it was clear that both boys and girls were holding high achievement in English. There is no significant difference in the achievement in English possessed by boys and girls.

The hypothesis that "there is a significant difference in the achievement in English of boy and girl of secondary school students" can be rejected as there is no significant difference in the achievement in English of boys and girls.

Hypothesis 2B

"There is a significant difference in the achievement in English of rural and urban secondary school students".

The validity of hypothesis was tested in the following manner.

There was a significant difference in the achievement in English of rural and urban secondary school students, though both of them possessed a high achievement in English. The rural students possessed higher achievement in English than their counterparts.

Table 4.8 Comparison of Achievement in English of Rural and Urban Secondary School Students

Variable	Sample	Mean	S.D.	M.D.	C.R.
Rural	143	97	8.21	2.22	2.46*
Urban	141	94.78	8.51		

* Significant at 0.05 level.

The hypothesis that "there is a significant difference in the achievement in English of rural and urban secondary school students" can be accepted as there is a significant difference in the achievement in English of rural and urban secondary school students.

Hypothesis 2C

"There is a significant difference in the achievement in English of government and private secondary school students".

The validity of hypothesis was tested in the following manner.

Table 4.9 Comparison of Achievement in English of Government and Private Secondary School Students

Variable	Sample	Mean	S.D.	M.D.	C.R.
Government	200	95	8.33	1.28	1.19*
Private	84	96.28	8.26		

* Not Significant at 0.05 level.

As can be seen from Table 4.9, both government and private school students were holding high achievement motivation without any significant difference between them.

The hypothesis that "there is a significant difference in the achievement in English of government and private secondary school students" can be rejected as there is no significant difference in the achievement in English of government and private secondary school students.

Hypothesis 2D

"There is a significant difference in the achievement in English reserved and unreserved caste secondary school students".

Table 4.10 Comparison of Achievement in English of Reserved and Unreserved Caste Secondary School Students

Variable	Sample	Mean	S.D.	M.D.	C.R.
Reserved	163	95.53	8.31	1.15	0.92*
Unreserved	121	96.68	9.21		

* Not significant at 0.05 level.

From Table 4.10, it can be seen that the reserved and unreserved caste students of secondary schools were holding high achievement in English without any significant difference between them.

The hypothesis that "there is a significant difference in the achievement in English of reserved and unreserved caste secondary school students" can be rejected as there is no significant difference in the achievement in English of reserved and unreserved caste secondary school students.

Hypothesis 3

"There is a positive correlation between achievement motivation and achievement in English of secondary school students".

To test the validity of hypothesis 3, the Pearson " value was computed.

There is a low positive correlation between achievement motivation and achievement in English in the secondary school students.

Table 4.11 Correlation between Achievement Motivation and Achievement in English in the Secondary School Students

Sample Size	Correlation between Achievement Motivation and Achievement in English (Pearson Value)
284	0.20

The hypothesis that "there is a positive correlation between achievement motivation and achievement in English of secondary school students" can be accepted as there is a positive correlation, though low, between achievement motivation and achievement in English of secondary school students.

Hypothesis 3A

"There is a positive correlation between achievement motivation and achievement in English of boy and girl secondary school students".

The association between achievement motivation and achievement in English of boys and girls was tried in the following way.

Table 4.12 Correlation between Achievement Motivation and Achievement in English in Boy and Girl Secondary School Students

Variable	Sample Size	Correlation between Achievement Motivation and Achievement in English (Pearson Value)
Boys	140	0.11
Girls	144	0.64

As per the table values, the correlation between achievement motivation and achievement in English was very low in boys and it was of middle level in Girls.

The hypothesis that "there is a positive correlation between achievement motivation and achievement in English of boy and girl secondary school students" can be accepted as there is a positive correlation between achievement motivation and achievement in English in both boys and girls.

Hypothesis 3B

"There is a positive correlation between achievement motivation and achievement in English of rural and urban secondary school students".

To test the validity of the hypothesis 3B, the Pearson " values were computed.

Table 4.13 Correlation between Achievement Motivation and Achievement in English of Rural and Urban Secondary School Students

Variable	Sample Size	Correlation between Achievement Motivation and Achievement in English (Pearson Value)
Rural	143	- 0.06
Urban	141	0.04

As per the values, the achievement motivation and achievement in English in rural secondary school students was negatively correlated and the achievement motivation and achievement in English in urban secondary school students was positively correlated at a very low level.

The hypothesis that "there is a positive correlation between achievement motivation and achievement in English of rural and urban secondary schools" can be rejected in case of rural secondary school students and can be accepted in case of urban secondary school students.

Hypothesis 3C

"There is a positive correlation between achievement motivation and achievement in English of private and government secondary school students."

To test the validity of hypothesis 3C, the Pearson " values were computed and they were given hereunder.

Table 4.14: Correlation between Achievement Motivation and Achievement in English of Government and Private Secondary School Students

Variable	Sample Size	Correlation between Achievement Motivation and Achievement in English (Pearson Value)
Government	200	0.13
Private	84	0.08

As per the table values, the achievement motivation and achievement in English in government and private secondary school students were correlated positively at a very low level.

The hypothesis that "there is a positive correlation between achievement motivation and achievement in English of private and government secondary school students" can be accepted as there is a low positive correlation between achievement motivation and achievement in English in both private and government secondary school students.

Hypothesis 3D

"There is a positive correlation between achievement motivation and achievement in English of reserved and unreserved caste secondary school students".

As per the table values, the correlation was very low and positive between achievement motivation and achievement in English in both reserved and unreserved caste secondary school students.

The hypothesis that "there is a positive correlation between achievement motivation and achievement in English of reserved and unreserved caste secondary school students" can be accepted as there is a very low positive correlation between achievement motivation and achievement in English of reserved and unreserved caste secondary school students.

Table 4.15 Correlation between Achievement Motivation and Achievement in English in Reserved and Unreserved Caste Secondary School Students

Variable	Sample Size	Correlation between Achievement Motivation and Achievement in English (Pearson Value)
Reserved	163	0.08
Unreserved	121	0.01

5 Summary, Conclusions Discussion and Suggestions

Gandhiji stated that "Education is drawing out of the best in child and man — body, mind and spirit". According to John Dewey "Education is the development of all those capacities in the individual, which will enable him to control his environment and fulfill his possibilities".

The need to achieve is the spring board of the achievement motive. In a competitive set up, the desire to excel over others or achieve a higher level than one's peers intensifies, which in turn may lead to a stronger motive to achieve something or every thing that is essential to beat others in the race and consequently experience a sense of pride and pleasure in the achievement. The type of motivation produced by such desire for achievement is called achievement motivation.

The subject English, as an important subject in the school curriculum, develops language and communicative skills, and enables students settle well in school and society. The achievement in English will help the teacher and student do well in the subject and take necessary remedial measures.

Identifying the very importance of achievement motivation and achievement in English in the student life, a study has been undertaken to study the level of achievement motivation and achievement in English and their relationship with each other at secondary school level.

The objectives of the present study were:

- ❖ To find out the level of achievement motivation of secondary school students;
- ❖ To find out the difference in the achievement motivation between boy and girl students, rural and urban school students, private and government school students, and reserved and unreserved caste students of secondary schools;
- ❖ To find out the level of achievement in English of secondary school students;
- ❖ To find out the difference in the achievement in English between boy and girl students, rural and urban school students, private and government school students, and reserved and unreserved caste students of secondary schools;
- ❖ To find out the correlation between achievement motivation and achievement in English of secondary school students;
- ❖ To find out the correlation between achievement motivation and achievement in English of boy and girl students, rural and school urban students, government and private school students, and reserved and unreserved caste students of secondary schools.

The normative survey method was used in the present study to realize the objectives of the study.

The variables considered for the study were secondary school boys *vs.* girls, rural secondary school students *vs.* urban secondary school students, private secondary school students *vs.* government secondary school students, and reserved caste *vs.* unreserved caste secondary school students.

The hypotheses formulated for the present study were:

1. The secondary school students are possessing high achievement motivation.

   1A. There is a significant difference in the achievement motivation of boy and girl students of secondary schools.

   1B. There is a significant difference in the achievement motivation of rural and urban secondary school students.

   1C. There is a significant difference in the achievement motivation of private and government secondary school students.

   1D. There is a significant difference in the achievement motivation of reserved and unreserved caste secondary school students.

2. The secondary school students are possessing high achievement in English.

   2A. There is a significant difference in the achievement in English of boy and girl secondary school students.

   2B. There is a significant difference in the achievement in English of rural and urban secondary school students.

   2C. There is a significant difference in the achievement in English of government and private secondary school students.

   2D. There is a significant difference in the achievement in English of reserved and unreserved caste secondary school students.

3. There is a positive correlation between achievement motivation and achievement in English of secondary school students.

3A. There is a positive correlation between achievement motivation and achievement in English of boy and girl secondary school students.

3B. There is a positive correlation between achievement motivation and achievement in English of rural and urban secondary school students.

3C. There is a positive correlation between achievement motivation and achievement in English of private and government secondary school students.

3D. There is a positive correlation between achievement motivation and achievement in English of reserved and unreserved caste secondary school students.

A sample of 284 was selected from the tenth class students studying in secondary schools of Guntur district by stratified random sampling technique.

Achievement Motivation Scale standardized by Beena Shah was used to collect the data regarding achievement motivation and the public examination marks obtained by the sample in English were collected from the respective schools of the sample to measure the achievement in English. These raw scores were used for data analysis.

The mean, standard deviation, critical ratio and Pearson correlation were calculated to identify the level of achievement motivation and achievement in English and their mutual correlation along with either to accept or reject the hypotheses formulated for verification.

Conclusions and Discussion

The following are the conclusions drawn from the analysis of data. These conclusions are followed by necessary discussion.

1. The secondary school students are holding high achievement motivation.

Achievement motivation is considered as the expectancy of satisfaction in mastering the challenging tasks. Very particularly, it is very essential in the field of education as it helps in academic excellence.

As the secondary school students are possessing high achievement motivation, they should utilise this motivation to enhance their academic achievement in different subjects that they are exposed in the school curriculum.

The teachers should provide opportunities and activities to enhance the achievement motivation of the secondary school students. The students should utilise the opportunities provided by the school in enhancing their achievement motivation. The parents or the guardians should help their children in achieving excellence in all academic activities by utilizing the achievement motivation in consultation with the school authorities and the teachers.

2. The secondary school boys and girls are possessing high achievement motivation without any significant difference between them.

The studies of Bhaskaran, Gandhi, Nagalakshmi, Gupta, Chauhan, Lalitha, Bharathi, and Jain found no difference in the achievement motivation of boys and girls. The study of Hari Krishna found that girls were with high achievement motivation than boys and it was opposite in the study of Gawande.

The present result is really an encouraging one though the maturity levels of boys and girls differ significantly at this adolescent age. As per the observations of psychologists, there should be some difference in their achievement motivation as the physical and psychological maturities and the exposure to social and academic affairs differ from boys to girls.

With the high achievement motivation, the secondary school boys and girls should strive to achieve better in school subjects.

3. The rural and urban secondary school students are possessing high achievement motivation with a significant difference between them. The rural students are with more academic achievement motivation than the urban students.

This result is supported by the study of Sharma and contradicted by the studies of Ahluwalia, Bhaskaran, and Saraswat. In the study of Gawande, the urban students were with high achievement motivation than rural students.

Though the academic facilities and the physical amenities available in urban areas are far superior to the rural areas, the rural secondary school students are with more achievement motivation than their counterparts. This may be the challenging nature of the rural students. It can also be assumed that the facilities that are enjoyed by the urban students put them in that level when compared to the rural students.

The rural and urban secondary school students with their high achievement motivation should try to enhance their academic achievement in every school subject.

4. The students studying in private and government secondary schools are possessing high achievement motivation with a significant difference between them. The private secondary school students are with more academic motivation than government secondary school students.

The studies of Ahluwalia and Bhaskaran found no difference in the achievement motivation between the students of private and government secondary schools.

The instructional and infrastructure facilities do not seem to have any influence on the achievement in English of private and government secondary school students though these facilities significantly differ from private schools to government schools. This may be due to the recognition of the importance of education by the students studying in these two kinds of schools.

The students of private and government secondary schools should continue to have the same kind of high achievement motivation, which helps in enhancing their academic performance in the curricular subjects.

5. **The reserved and unreserved caste secondary school students are having high achievement motivation with a significant difference between them. The reserved caste students are with low achievement motivation than unreserved caste students.**

Dutt found a high achievement motivation in tribal (reserved caste) students.

In the society, the unreserved caste students along with their families are advanced in terms of financial and social status when compared to the reserved caste students. With this background only, the caste reservations are in force in the society to bring forth the reserved caste communities on par with unreserved communities by providing reservations in admissions and employment and by providing financial support and other benefits. The reserved community students should utilize the free facilities and opportunities provided by the government and other agencies.

Both reserved and unreserved caste students should make use of this high achievement motivation in enhancing their academic performance in the school.

6. **The secondary school students are holding high achievement in English.**

The high achievement in English possessed by the secondary school students is really a good sign in the academics of the schools. This high achievement in English may be helpful to the secondary school students to pursue higher education and or professional courses with ease and effect.

The secondary school students should continue the same in higher levels of learning also where ever and whenever they are supposed to learn the high language.

7. The secondary school boys and girls are with a high achievement in English without any significant difference between them.

Hari Krishnan, Mazumdar, and Rani observed a gender difference in achievement and Singh found no gender difference in achievement.

This high achievement in English in both boys and girls states that the gender does not play any role in achievement in English, though the physical and psychological maturities differ significantly in boys and girls at this adolescent stage. This is a good symbol per enhancing the achievement in English at secondary school level without bothering about the gender difference.

Both boys and girls should continue the same type of academic achievement in every academic subject without worrying about their gender benefits and deficiencies.

8. The rural and urban secondary school students are holding high achievement in English with a significant difference. The rural students are holding high achievement in English than urban students.

Shahapur found a significant difference and Manju Singh found no significant difference in the academic achievement of boys and girls. Singh, Bhaskaran, and Nagaraju et. al. observed high achievement in urban students than rural students.

The difference in the achievement in English of rural and urban secondary school students strongly states that the rural students are doing their best to compete with urban students in every academic aspect even though the rural students help the families by attending to various domestic activities when compared with their counterparts.

Though there is a significant difference in the achievement in English of rural and urban secondary school students, they should further work hard to get good scores in their examinations with equal status. If the students identify the reasons for the difference in their achievement, they can overcome them and get good scores equally.

9. The students studying in government and private secondary schools are with high achievement in English without any significant difference between them.

The studies of Ahluwalia, and Bhaskaran found no significant difference in the achievement of government and private secondary schools.

Inspite of the significant differences in the infrastructure and instructional facilities present in the government and private secondary schools, the students of these schools scored very high marks in English with equal status. This indicates that the facilities may not influence the achievement if the students do try well to achieve well in school subjects.

The students studying in private and government secondary schools should continue the same in future also recognising the importance of excellent academic performance.

10. The reserved and unreserved caste secondary school students are with high achievement in English without any significant difference between them.

Irrespective of the advantages and limitations that either a reserved caste or a unreserved caste carry on, both the reserved and unreserved caste secondary school students achieved very well in English with no difference between them. This result indicates that the caste benefits and drawbacks do not have any influence on the academic achievement of students. Now-a-days, every student from any financial or social background is mostly committed to achieve well in education as he/she knows the benefits associated with better academic advancement.

All the students ignoring their social status should do well in every examination to have a better and lucrative employment and life.

11. The correlation between achievement motivation and achievement in English is low and positive in secondary school students.

Usually, the high achievement motivation promotes high achievement in curricular subjects. Though there is no high significant positive correlation between achievement motivation and achievement in English, there is a positive correlation between them. This should help the students achieve well in all school subjects, along with English.

12. The correlation between achievement motivation and achievement in English is low and positive in boys and middle and positive in girls who are studying in secondary schools.

The studies of Chandy, Fatmi, and Gawande revealed a significant correlation between achievement motivation and achievement and gender. Fatmi found higher correlation in girls, but Gawade found higher correlation in boys.

The positive but different levels of positive correlation between achievement motivation and achievement in English in boys and girls may be due to the involvement of these students in various academic activities at home and school. The high correlation in girls than boys between achievement motivation and achievement in English may also be due to psychological maturity, aptitude, attitude and interests in the subjects.

13. The achievement motivation is correlated with achievement in English negatively at a very low level in rural secondary school students and achievement motivation is correlated positively with achievement in English at a very low level.

The correlation between achievement motivation and achievement in English may be either positive or negative is very low in urban secondary school students and rural secondary school students. These correlations are very negligible and can be considered that one is not influencing much the other either way.

14. The correlation between achievement motivation and achievement in English is positive at a very low level in the government and private secondary school students.

The level of positive correlation between achievement motivation and achievement in English need to be more in both government and private secondary school students in order to enhance more their achievement levels in school subjects.

15. The correlation between achievement motivation and achievement in English in both reserved caste and unreserved caste secondary school students is very low and positive.

The correlation between achievement motivation and achievement in English need to be more in both reserved and unreserved caste students in order to enhance the level of academic achievement with the existing high achievement motivation.

The major findings of the present study on the achievement motivation and achievement in English of secondary school students are:

❖ The secondary school students are holding high achievement motivation.

- There is a significant difference in the achievement motivation of rural and urban school students, government and private school students, and reserved and unreserved caste students, except in boys and girls where there is no significant difference in their achievement motivation.
- Secondary school students are possessing a high achievement in English.
- There is no significant difference between boys and girls, government and private school students, and reserved and unreserved caste students in achievement in English, except in rural and urban secondary school students where there is a significant difference between them in achievement in English.
- There is a very low positive correlation between achievement motivation and achievement in English in secondary school students.
- The correlation between achievement motivation and achievement in English is positively correlated at middle level; is correlated positively at a very low level in boys, urban students, government school students, private school students, reserved caste students and unreserved caste students; and is negatively correlated at a very low level in rural students.

Suggestions for Further Research

The following studies may be considered for research by the investigators:

- This type of studies may be extended to college, university and professional institutions.
- The influence of personality factors on achievement motivation and achievement (in various subjects) may be studied.

- The psycho correlates of achievement motivation and achievement in English (or other subjects) may be considered for research.
- The relationship among achievement motivation, achievement in English (or other subjects) and socio-economic status of students may be studied.

Bibliography

Agarwal, J.C. (1999). *Essentials of Educational Technology,* Teaching Learning Innovations in Education. New Delhi: Vikas Publishing House Pvt. Ltd.

Aggarwal, J.C. (1993). *Development and Planning of Modern Education,* 4th Edition. New Delhi: Vikas Publishing Pvt. Ltd.

Aggarwal, J.C. (1994). *Essentials of Educational Psychology.* New Delhi: Vikas Publshing House Pvt. Ltd.

Aggarwal, J.C., Aggarwal, S.P. (1989). *National Policy on Education.* New Delhi: Concept Publishing Company.

Atkinson, J., Berna, E. and Woodworth, R.S. (1988). *Dictionary of Psychology,* 4th Edition. New Delhi: Goyal Saab Publishers.

Baskara Rao, Digumarti (1997). *Scientific Attitude.* New Delhi: Discovery Publishing House.

Baskara Rao, Digumarti (2004). *Scientific Attitude, Scientific Aptitude and Achievement in Biology.* New Delhi: Discovery Publishing House.

Baskara Rao, Editor (1998). *Reforming School Education.* New Delhi: Discovery Publishing House.

Best, John W. and James V. Khan (2005). *Research in Education*, 9th Edition. New Delhi: Prentice-Hall of India Private Limited.

Bhatia and Bhatia (1984). *The Philosophical and Sociologial Foundations of Education*, 5th Edition. Delhi: Doaba House.

Bhatia, B.D. and Safaya, R.N. *Educational Psychology and Guidance*. Delhi : Dhanpat Rai and Sons.

Bhatiya and Bhatiya (1996). *A Text Book of Educational Psychology*. New Delhi: Doaba House.

Bhatiya, H.R. (1977). *A Text Book of Educational Psychology*. New Delhi: MacMillan India Ltd.

Bipin Asthana and Agarwal (1991). *Measurement and Evaluation in Psychology and Education*, 4th Edition. Agra: Vind Prakash Mandir.

Buch, M.B., (Editor) (1974). *A Survey of Research in Education*. Baroda: M.S. University.

Buch, M.B., Editor (1978-1983). *Third Survey of Research in Education*. Baroda: CASE, M.S. University of Baroda.

Buch, M.B., Editor (1983-1988). *Fourth Survey of Reseach of Education*. New Delhi: NCERT.

Chaube, S.P. (1983). *Educational Psychology*. Agra: Printsman.

Chauhan, S.S. (1978). *Advanced Educational Psychology*. New Delhi: Vikas Publishing House.

Crow, L.D. and Crow, A. (1991). *Educational Psychology*. New Delhi: Eurasia Publishing House Pvt. Ltd.

Dosajh, N.L. (1982). *Advanced Educational Psychology*. New Delhi: Allied Publishers Pvt. Ltd.

Garret, M.E. *Statistical in Psychology and Education*. Hyderabad: International Book Bureau.

Hariss, Chester W. (1960). *Encyclopaedia of Educational Research*, 3rd Edition. New York: The MacMillan Co.

Hurlock, Elizabeth (1992). *Development Psychology, A Life-span Approach,* Fifth Edition, Bombay: Tata McGraw-Hill Publishing Co. Ltd.

Husen Torsten, Neville Postlethwaite (1985). *The International Encyclopaedia of Education,* Vol. 3 D.E., Vol.4, F-H. England: Pergamon Press Ltd.

Jagannath, Mohanty (2004). *Modern Trends in Educational Technology.* Hyderabad: Neelkamal Publications Pvt. Ltd.

Jyosthana, M. and Nageswara Rao (2010). *Methods of Teaching English.* Guntur : Sri Nagarjuna Publishers, master minds.

Kulbir Singh Siddhu (1990). *Methodology of Research in Education.* New Delhi: Sterling Publishers Pvt. Ltd.

Kuppu, Swami (2003). *Advanced Educational Psychology.* New Delhi: Sterling Publishers Pvt. Ltd.

Lokesh, Koul (1984). *Methodology of Educational Research.* New Delhi: Vikas Publishing House Pvt. Ltd.

Mangal, S.K. (1989). *Abnormal Psychology.* New Delhi: Sterling Publishers Pvt. Ltd.

Mangal, S.K. (1998). *Psychological Foundations of Education.* Ludhiana: Prakash Brothers.

Mangal, S.K. (2004). *Statistics in Educational and Psychology,* 2nd Edition. New Delhi: Prentice-Hall of India Pvt. Ltd.

Mathur, S.S. (1983). *Educational Psychology.* Agra: Vinod Prakash Mandir.

Murthy, S.K. (1983). *Essentials of Educational Psychology.* Ludhiana: Prakash Brothers.

Murthy, S.K. (1984). *Educational Technology.* Ludhiana: Prakash Brothers.

Safaya, R.N. and Bhatia, B.D. *Educational Psychology and Guidance.* New Delhi: Dhanpat Rai and Sons.

Sharma, R.N. (1992). *Principles and Techniques of Education*. New Delhi: Surjeet Publications.

Siddhu, Kulbir Singh (1990). *Methodology of Research in Education*. New Delhi: Sterling Publishers Private Limited.

Srinivastava, D.M. (1985). *Abnormal Psychology*. Agra: Vinod Pustak Mandir.

Srinivastava, D.N. (1985). *General Psychology*. Agra: Vinod Pustak Mandir.

Usha Rao (1997). *Educational Technology*. Mumbai: Himalaya Publishing House.

Withing Arno, F. and Gurney, Williams III (1984). *Psychology — An Introduction*. New York: Fony and Sons Prentery Priate Limited.

Yakaiah, P. and Bhatiya, K.E. (2003). *Introduction to Educational Psychology*. New Delhi: Kalyani Publications.

Young, Pauline V. (1988). *Scientific Social Surveys and Research*, 4th Edition. New Delhi: Prentice-Hall of India Pvt. Ltd.

Additional Reading

Bhaskara Rao, Digumarti (1994). *Scientific Aptitude*. New Delhi: Ashish Publishing House. ISBN 81-7024-658-X.

Bhaskara Rao, Digumarti (1995). *Animal Kingdom*. New Delhi: Discovery Publishing House. ISBN 81-7141-274-2.

Bhaskara Rao, Digumarti (1995). *Batracology*. New Delhi: Discovery Publishing House. ISBN 81-7141-279-3.

Bhaskara Rao, Digumarti (1997). *Scientific Attitude*. New Delhi: Discovery Publishing House. ISBN 81-7141-381-1.

Bhaskara Rao, Digumarti (1996). *Scientific Attitude vis-à-vis Scientific Aptitude*. New Delhi: Discovery Publishing House. ISBN 81-7141-308-0.

Bhaskara Rao, Digumarti (2004). *Scientific Attitude, Scientific Aptitude and Achievement*. New Delhi: Discovery Publishing House. ISBN 81-7141-781-7.

Bhaskara Rao, Digumarti (2004). *Educational Administration.* New Delhi: Discovery Publishing House. ISBN 81-7141-842-2.

Bhaskara Rao, Digumarti (2004). *Issues in School Education.* New Delhi: Discovery Publishing House, New Delhi. ISBN 81-8356-025-3.

Bhaskara Rao, Digumarti, Editor (1996). *Encyclopaedia of Education For All,* 5 Volumes. New Delhi: APH Publishing Corporation. ISBN 81-7024-759-4 (set).

Vol. I *Education For All: The World Conference.* ISBN 81-7024-760-8

Vol. II *Education For All: The EPA-9 Summit.* ISBN 81-7024-761-6.

Vol. III *Education For All: Quality Education For All.* ISBN 81-7024-762-6.

Vol. IV *Education for All: Planning and Monitoring.* ISBN 81-7024-763-4.

Vol. V *Education For All: The Indian Scenario.* ISBN 81-7024-764-0.

Bhaskara Rao, Digumarti, Editor (1999). *International Encyclopaedia of AIDS,* 11 volumes. New Delhi: Discovery Publishing House. ISBN 81-7141-522-6 (set).

Vol. 1 *Introduction to HIV/AIDS.* ISBN 81-7141-523-7.

Vol. 2 *HIV/AIDS — Issues and Challenges,* 2 parts. ISBN 81-7141-524-5.

Vol. 3 *HIV/AIDS — Socio Economic Realities.* ISBN 81-7141-524-3.

Vol. 4 *HIV/AIDS — Law Ethics and Human Rights,* 2 parts. ISBN 81-7141-526-1.

Vol. 5 *AIDS and NGOs.* ISBN 81-7141-527-X.

Vol. 6 *AIDS and Home Care.* ISBN 81-7141-528-8.

Vol. 7 *STD Case Management.* ISBN 81-7141-529-6.

Vol. 8 *HIV/AIDS Prevention and Care — Teaching Modules for Nurses and Midwives.* ISBN 81-7141-530-X.

Vol. 9 *HIV Prevention Education for Educational Institutions*. ISBN 81-7141-531-8.

Vol. 10 *Instructional Modules for AIDS Education*. ISBN 81-7141-532-6.

Vol. 11 *School Health Education to Prevent AIDS and STD — A Package for Curriculum Planners*. ISBN 81-7141-533-4.

Bhaskara Rao, Digumarti, Editor (2000). *International Encyclopaedia of Human Rights*, 7 volumes in 13 parts. New Delhi: Discovery Publishing House. ISBN 81-7141-567-9 (set).

Vol. 1 *International Instruments of Human Rights*, 2 parts. ISBN 81-7141-569-4.

Vol. 2 *Regional Instruments of Human Rights*. ISBN 81-7141-604-7.

Vol. 3 *Human Rights and the United Nations*, 2 parts. ISBN 81-7141-605-5.

Vol. 4 *Fact Files of Human Rights*, 3 parts. ISBN 81-7141-606-3.

Vol. 5 *Study Stories of Human Rights*, 3 parts. ISBN 81-7141-607-3.

Vol. 6 *International Meetings on Human Rights*, 2 parts. ISBN 81-7141-608-X.

Vol. 7 *Professional Training in Human Rights*. ISBN 81-7141-609-8.

Bhaskara Rao, Digumarti, Editor (2000). *International Encyclopaedia of Science and Technology Education*, 11 volumes. New Delhi: Discovery Publishing House. ISBN 81-7141-548-2 (set).

Vol. 1 *Science and Technology Education*. ISBN 81-7141-568-7.

Vol. 2 *Science Education in Developing Countries*. ISBN 81-7141-569-9.

Vol. 3 *Organizational Structure of Science.* ISBN 81-7141-570-9.

Vol. 4 *Science Education in Asia and the Pacific.* ISBN 81-7141-571-7

Vol. 5 *Science and Technology Education For All.* ISBN 81-7141-572-5.

Vol. 6 *Values, Ethics, Talent and Girls in Science and Technology Education.* ISBN 81-7141-573-3.

Vol. 7 *Popularization of Science and Technology Education.* ISBN 81-7141-574-1.

Vol. 8 *Science, Power and Society.* ISBN 81-7141- 575-X.

Vol. 9 *Information Technology.* ISBN 81-7141-576-8.

Vol. 10 *Teacher Training in Science and Technology Education.* ISBN 81-7142-577-6.

Vol. 11 *Teacher Training in Science and Technology: A Curriculum Framework.* ISBN 81-7141-578-4.

Bhaskara Rao, Digumarti, Editor (2000). *Education For All: Achieving the Goal,* 3 Volumes. New Delhi: APH Publishing Corporation. ISBN 81-7648-152-1 (set).

Vol. I *The Global Consensus.* ISBN 81-7648-155-6.

Vol. II *Mid-Decade Review Reports of Regional Seminars.* ISBN 81-7648-154-8.

Vol. III *Issues and Trends.* ISBN 81-7648-155-6.

Bhaskara Rao, Digumarti, Editor (2004). *International Encyclopaedia of Learning to Live Together,* 4 Volumes. New Delhi: Discovery Publishing House. ISBN 81-7141-848-1.

Vol. 1 *International Conference on Learning to Live Together.*

Vol. 2 *Globalization and Living Together.*

Vol. 3 *Curriculum for Learning to Live Together.*

Vol. 4 *Science Education for the Contemporary Society.*

Bhaskara Rao, Digumarti, Editor (2005). *Encyclopaedia of Education For All*, 3 volumes. New Delhi: Discovery Publishing House. ISBN 81-7141-647-0 (set).

Bhaskara Rao, Digumarti, Editor (2007). *Encyclopaedia of Teacher Education*, 4 volumes. New Delhi: Discovery Publishing House. ISBN 81-8356-306-6 (set).

Bhaskara Rao, Digumarti, Editor (2007). *Encyclopaedia of Edeucation for Living Together*, 4 volumes. New Delhi: Discovery Publishing House. ISBN 81-7141-848-1 (set).

Bhaskara Rao, Digumarti, Editor (1996). *National Policy on Education*, 2 Volumes. New Delhi: Anmol Publications Pvt. Ltd. ISBN 81-7488-323-1.

Bhaskara Rao, Digumarti, Editor (1996). *Global Perceptions on Peace Education*, 3 volumes. New Delhi: Discovery Publishing House. ISBN 81-7141-319-6.

Bhaskara Rao, Digumarti, Editor (1997). *Education for the 21st Century*. New Delhi: Discovery Publishing House. ISBN 81-7141-389-7.

Bhaskara Rao, Digumarti, Editor (1997). *Reflections on Scientific Attitude*. New Delhi: Discovery Publishing House. ISBN 81-7141-319-6.

Bhaskara Rao, Digumarti, Editor (1997). *Success Story of a Primary Education Project*. New Delhi: APH Publishing Corporation. ISBN 81-7024-850-7.

Bhaskara Rao, Digumarti, Editor (1997). *World Food Summit*. New Delhi: Discovery Publishing House. ISBN 81-7141-386-2.

Bhaskara Rao, Digumarti, Editor (1997). *Care the Child*, 2 volumes. New Delhi: Discovery Publishing House. ISBN 81-7141-394-3.

Bhaskara Rao, Digumarti, Editor (1998). *Earth Summit*, 2 volumes. New Delhi: Discovery Publishing House. ISBN 81-7141-435-4.

Bhaskara Rao, Digumarti, Editor (1998). *Adolescence Education.* New Delhi: Discovery Publishing House. ISBN 81-7141-432-X.

Bhaskara Rao, Digumarti, Editor (1998). *Community and School Nutrition Education.* New Delhi: Discovery Publishing House. ISBN 81-7141-435-4.

Bhaskara Rao, Digumarti, Editor (1998). *District Primary Education Programme.* New Delhi: Discovery Publishing House. ISBN 81-7141-396-X.

Bhaskara Rao, Digumarti, Editor (1998). *National Policy on Education: Towards an Enlightened and Humane Society.* New Delhi: Discovery Publishing House. ISBN 81-7141-426-5.

Bhaskara Rao, Digumarti, Editor (1998). *Reforming School Education.* New Delhi: Discovery Publishing House. ISBN 81-7141-403-6.

Bhaskara Rao, Digumarti, Editor (1998). *Teacher Education in India.* New Delhi: Discovery Publishing House. ISBN 81-7141-406-0.

Bhaskara Rao, Digumarti, Editor (1998). *World Summit for Social Development.* New Delhi: Discovery Publishing House. ISBN 81-7141-420-6.

Bhaskara Rao, Digumarti, Editor (2001). *Nuclear Materials: Issues and Concerns,* 2 volumes. New Delhi: Discovery Publishing House. ISBN 81-7141-611-X.

Bhaskara Rao, Digumarti, Editor (2001). *Distance Education in Different Countries.* New Delhi: APH Publishing Corporation. ISBN 81-7648-229-3.

Bhaskara Rao, Digumarti, Editor (2001). *Decentralised Management of Education: Management of Education in Panchayati Raj and Municipal Bodies.* New Delhi: Discovery Publishing House. ISBN 81-7141-617-9.

Bhaskara Rao, Digumarti, Editor (2001). *Electrochemistry for Environmental Protection.* New Delhi: Discovery Publishing House. ISBN 81-7141-619-5.

Bhaskara Rao, Digumarti, Editor (2001). *Global Educational Studies*. New Delhi: Discovery Publishing House. ISBN 81-7141-616-0.

Bhaskara Rao, Digumarti, Editor (2001). *Global Synthesis of Educational Assessment*. New Delhi: Discovery Publishing House. ISBN 81-7141-613-6.

Bhaskara Rao, Digumarti, Editor (2001). *Jomtein Decade of Education*. New Delhi: Discovery Publishing House. ISBN 81-7141-618-7.

Bhaskara Rao, Digumarti, Editor (2001). *World Conference on Education for All*. New Delhi: APH Publishing Corporation. ISBN 81-7141-274-9.

Bhaskara Rao, Digumarti, Editor (2001). *World Conference on Higher Education*. New Delhi: Discovery Publishing House. ISBN 81-7141-610-1.

Bhaskara Rao, Digumarti, Editor (2001). *World Conference on Science*. New Delhi: Discovery Publishing House. ISBN 81-7141-612-8.

Bhaskara Rao, Digumarti, Editor (2003). *Inspiring Experiences in Teacher Education*. New Delhi: Discovery Publishing House. ISBN 81-7141-656-X.

Bhaskara Rao, Digumarti, Editor (2003). *International Studies in Education*, 3 Volumes. New Delhi: Discovery Publishing House. ISBN 81-7141-647-0.

Bhaskara Rao, Digumarti, Editor (2003). *Military Conversion: Impact on Science and Technology*. New Delhi: Discovery Publishing House. ISBN 81-7141-578-4.

Bhaskara Rao, Digumarti, Editor (2003). *United Nations Millennium Summit*. New Delhi: Discovery Publishing House. ISBN 81-7141-632-2.

Bhaskara Rao, Digumarti, Editor (2003). *World Assembly on Aging*. New Delhi: Discovery Publishing House. ISBN 81-7141-637-3.

Bhaskara Rao, Digumarti, Editor (2003). *World Conference on Human Rights.* New Delhi: Discovery Publishing House. ISBN 81-7141-661-6.

Bhaskara Rao, Digumarti, Editor (2003). *World Education Forum.* New Delhi: Discovery Publishing House. ISBN 81-7141-639-X.

Bhaskara Rao, Digumarti, Editor (2003). *Education, Employment and Human Resource Development.* New Delhi: Discovery Publishing House. ISBN 81-7141-681-0.

Bhaskara Rao, Digumarti, Editor (2003). *Successful Schooling.* New Delhi: Discovery Publishing House. ISBN 81-7141-677-2.

Bhaskara Rao, Digumarti, Editor (2003). *European Education and Teachers.* New Delhi: Discovery Publishing House. ISBN 81-7141-702-7.

Bhaskara Rao, Digumarti, Editor (2003). *Teachers in a Changing World.* New Delhi: Discovery Publishing House. ISBN 81-7141-694-2.

Bhaskara Rao, Digumarti, Editor (2004). *International Guidelines on Open and Distance Teacher Education.* New Delhi: Discovery Publishing House. ISBN 81-7141-777-9.

Bhaskara Rao, Digumarti, Editor (2004). *Adult Learning in the 21st Century.* New Delhi: Discovery Publishing House. ISBN 81-7141-797-3.

Bhaskara Rao, Digumarti, Editor (2004). *Educational Practices: Research and Recommendations.* New Delhi: Discovery Publishing House. ISBN 81-7141-835-X.

Bhaskara Rao, Digumarti, Editor (2004). *General Secondary Education in the 21st Century.* New Delhi: Discovery Publishing House.

Bhaskara Rao, Digumarti, Editor (2004). *Reforming Secondary Education.* New Delhi: Discovery Publishing House. ISBN 81-7141-843-0.

Bhaskara Rao, Digumarti, Editor (2004). *Human Rights Education*. New Delhi: Discovery Publishing House. ISBN 81-7141-882-1.

Bhaskara Rao, Digumarti, Editor (2004). *United Nations Decade for Human Rights Education*. New Delhi: Discovery Publishing House. ISBN 81-7141-887-2.

Bhaskara Rao, Digumarti, Editor (2004). *Technical and Vocational Education and Training in the 21st Century*. New Delhi: Discovery Publishing House. ISBN 81-7141- 984-4.

Bhaskara Rao, Digumarti, Editor (2005). *Encyclopaedia of Education For All*, 3 Volumes. New Delhi: Discovery Publishing House.

Bhaskara Rao, Digumarti, Editor (2011). *Right to Education*. Hyderabad: Neel Kamal Publishers.

Bhaskara Rao, Digumarti, Editor (2011). *International Encyclopaedia of Educational Policies*. Hyderabad: Neel Kamal Publishers.

Bhaskara Rao, Digumarti, Editor (2011). *International Encyclopaedia of Educational Practices*. Hyderabad: Neel Kamal Publishers.

Bhaskara Rao, Digumarti and B.S.V. Dutt, Editors (2003). *Education: Programmes and Policies*. New Delhi: APH Publishing Corporation. ISBN 81-7648-470-9.

Bhaskara Rao, Digumarti, C.A.P. Swamy and B.S.V. Dutt (1997). *Self-Evaluation in Student Teaching*. New Delhi: Discovery Publishing House. ISBN 81-7141-374-9.

Bhaskara Rao, Digumarti and C.D. Swarna Latha, Editors (2006). *Encyclopaedia of Biotechnology*, 5 volumes. New Delhi: Discovery Publishing House. ISBN 81-8356-168-3 (set).

Bhaskara Rao, Digumarti, C. Sridevi and K. Vijaya (1995). *Achievement in Social Studies*. New Delhi: Discovery Publishing House. ISBN 81-7141-281-5.

Bhaskara Rao, Digumarti and D. Naresh Kumar (2004). *School Teacher Effectiveness*. New Delhi: Discovery Publishing House. ISBN 81-7141-782-5.

Bhaskara Rao, Digumarti and D. Sridhar (2002). *Job Satisfaction of School Teachers.* New Delhi: Discovery Publishing House. ISBN 81-7141-652-7.

Bhaskara Rao, Digumarti and Digumarti Pushpa Latha, Editors (1998). *International Encyclopaedia of Women,* 5 volumes. New Delhi: Discovery Publishing House. ISBN 81-7141-410-9 (set).

Vol. 1 *Status of World's Women.* ISBN 81-7141- 494-X.

Vol. 2 *Women, Education and Empowerment.* ISBN 81-7141-498-1.

Vol. 3 *Women Challenges and Advancement.* ISBN 81-7141-497-4.

Vol. 4 *Women and Family Health.* ISBN 81-7141- 497-4.

Vol. 5 *Women and International Action.* ISBN 81-7141-498-2.

Bhaskara Rao, Digumarti and Digumarti Pushpa Latha (1994). *Achievement in Biology.* New Delhi: Discovery Publishing House. ISBN 81-7141-264-5.

Bhaskara Rao, Digumarti and Digumarti Pushpa Latha (1995). *Achievement in English.* New Delhi: Discovery Publishing House. ISBN 81-7141-283-1.

Bhaskara Rao, Digumarti and Digumarti Pushpa Latha (1994). *Achievement in Science.* New Delhi: Discovery Publishing House. ISBN 81-7141-280-70.

Bhaskara Rao, Digumarti and Digumarti Pushpa Latha (1995). *Achievement in Mathematics.* New Delhi: Discovery Publishing House. ISBN 81-7141-278-5.

Bhaskara Rao, Digumarti and Digumarti Pushpa Latha (2004). *Education for Women.* New Delhi: Discovery Publishing House. ISBN 81-7141-873-2.

Bhaskara Rao, Digumarti, Digumarti Pushpa Latha and Digumarthi Harshitha, Editors (2001). *Biological Warfare.* New Delhi: Discovery Publishing House. ISBN 81-7141-597-0.

Bhaskara Rao, Digumarti, Digumarti Pushpa Latha and Digumarthi Harshitha, Editors (2001). *Women As Educators*. New Delhi: Discovery Publishing House. ISBN 81-7141-602-0.

Bhaskara Rao, Digumarti and Digumarthi Harshitha (2004). *Adjustment of Adolescents*. New Delhi: APH Publishing House. ISBN 81-7648-836-8.

Bhaskara Rao, Digumarti and Digumarthi Harshitha, Editors (2001). *Education in India*. New Delhi: APH Publishing House. ISBN 81-7648-207-2.

Bhaskara Rao, Digumarti, Digumarti Pushpa Latha and Digumarthi Harshitha, Editors (2001). *Assessing Learning Achievement*. New Delhi: Discovery Publishing House. ISBN 81-7141-601-2.

Bhaskara Rao, Digumarti, Digumarti Pushpa Latha and Digumarthi Harshitha, Editors (2001). *Energy Security*. New Delhi: Discovery Publishing House. ISBN 81-7141-598-9.

Bhaskara Rao, Digumarti, Digumarthi Harshitha and K.R.S. Sambasiva Rao, Editors (1999). *Advanced Biotechnology*. New Delhi: Discovery Publishing House. ISBN 81-7141-516-4.

Bhaskara Rao, Digumarti and K.R.S. Sambasiva Rao, Editors (1996). *Current Trends in Indian Education*. New Delhi: Discovery Publishing House. ISBN 81-7141-311-0.

Bhaskara Rao, Digumarti and D. Naresh Kumar (2004). *School Teacher Effectiveness*. New Delhi: Discovery Publishing House. ISBN 81-7141-782-5.

Bhaskara Rao, Digumarti and E. Sreekanth Babu (2004). *Educational Interests of School Students*. New Delhi: Discovery Publishing House. ISBN 81-7141-837-6.

Bhaskara Rao, Digumarti and K. Vijaya (1995). *A Text Book Evaluation*. Ambala Cantt: The Associated Publishers.

Bhaskara Rao, Digumarti and M.A. Fayaz (2004). *Problems of Primary School Drop-outs.* New Delhi: Discovery Publishing House. ISBN 81-7141- 834-1.

Bhaskara Rao, Digumarti and N.V.M. Mohana Rao (2002). *Problems of Mentally Handicapped Children.* New Delhi: Discovery Publishing House. ISBN 81-7141- 645-4.

Bhaskara Rao, Digumarti and S. Chandra Mohan (2002). *Sports Management.* New Delhi: APH Publishing House. ISBN 81-7648-467-9.

Bhaskara Rao, Digumarti and S.A. Khader (2004). *Problems of Private School Teachers.* New Delhi: Discovery Publishing House. ISBN 81-7141-838-4.

Bhaskara Rao, Digumarti and S.A. Khader (2004). *School Education in India.* New Delhi: Discovery Publishing House. ISBN 81-7141-849-X.

Bhaskara Rao, Digumarti and Sk. Johni Basha (2004). *Teachers' Population Education Awareness.* New Delhi: Discovery Publishing House. ISBN 81-7141-832-5.

Bhaskara Rao, Digumarti, V.V. Rao, V.V. Lakshmi and V.V. Krishna, Editors (1999). *Status and Advancement of Women.* New Delhi: APH Publishing House. ISBN 81-7648-169-6.

Appala Naidu, P.Ch., Author and Digumarti Bhaskara Rao, Editor (2007). *Feedback Methods and Students Performance.* New Delhi: Discovery Publishing House. ISBN 81-8356-284-1.

Babu, P.C., Author and Digumarti Bhaskara Rao, Editor (2004). *Flowers of Wisdom.* New Delhi: Discovery Publishing House. ISBN 81-7141-695-0.

Bujji Babu, K., Author and Digumarti Bhaskara Rao, Editor (2007). *Teaching Aptitude of Primary School Teachers.* New Delhi: Sonali Publications. ISBN 81-8411-083-9.

Amala, P.A. and Anupama, P., Authors and Digumarti Bhaskara Rao, Editor (2004). *History of Education.* New Delhi: Discovery Publishing House. ISBN 81-7141-860-0.

Bhagya Lakshmi, L., Author and Digumarti Bhaskara Rao, Editor (2000). *Reading and Comprehension.* New Delhi: Discovery Publishing House. ISBN 81-7141-543-1.

Bhasha, S.A., Author and Digumarti Bhaskara Rao, Editor (2004). *Methods of Teaching Geography.* New Delhi: Discovery Publishing House. ISBN 81-7141-807-4.

Bhuvaneswara Lakshmi, Gadde, Author and Digumarti Bhaskara Rao, Editor(2000). *Attitude Towards Science.* New Delhi: Discovery Publishing House. ISBN 81-7141-541-6.

Bhuvaneswara Lakshmi, G., Author and Digumarti Bhaskara Rao, Editor (2004). *Methods of Teaching Life Science.* New Delhi: Discovery Publishing House. ISBN 81-7141-804-X.

Bhuvaneswara Lakshmi, G. and K. Subba Rao, Authors and Digumarti Bhaskara Rao, Editor (2004). *Methods of Teaching Biology.* New Delhi: Discovery Publishing House. ISBN 81-7141-914-3.

Chary, K.V.N.B., Author and Digumarti Bhaskara Rao, Editor (2006). *Techniques of Teaching Physics.* New Delhi: Sonali Publications. ISBN 81-8411-046-4.

Chowdary, S.B.J.R. and Naga Raju, Authors and Digumarti Bhaskara Rao, Editor (2004). *Mastery of Teaching Skills.* New Delhi: Discovery Publishing House. ISBN 81-7141-861-9.

Dayakara Reddy, V. and Digumarti Bhaskara Rao, Editors (2006). *Value-oriented Education.* New Delhi: Discovery Publishing House. ISBN 81-8356-051-2.

Devraj, T.A.S., Author and Digumarti Bhaskara Rao, Editor (1997). *Trace Analysis of Uranium and Thorium.* New Delhi: Discovery Publishing House. ISBN 81-7141-375-7.

Durga Rani, K., Author and Digumarti Bhaskara Rao, Editor (2000). *Educational Aspirations and Scientific Attitudes.* New Delhi: Discovery Publishing House. ISBN 81-7141-555-5.

Dutt, B.S.V. and Digumarti Bhaskara Rao (2001). *Empowering Primary Teachers.* New Delhi: Discovery Publishing House. ISBN 81-7141-615-2.

Dutt, B.S.V., Author and Digumarti Bhaskara Rao, Editor (2004). *Comparative Education.* New Delhi: Discovery Publishing House. ISBN 81-7141-912-7.

Ediger, Marlow and Digumarti Bhaskara Rao, Editors (2006). *Encyclopaedia of School Education,* 5 volumes. New Delhi: Discovery Publishing House. ISBN 81-8356-308-2 (set).

Ediger, Marlow and Digumarti Bhaskara Rao, Editors (2006). *Encyclopaedia of School Administration,* 4 volumes. New Delhi: Discovery Publishing House. ISBN 81-8356-307-4 (set).

Ediger, Marlow and Digumarti Bhaskara Rao, Editors (2007). *Encyclopaedia of School Curriculum,* 10 volumes. New Delhi: Discovery Publishing House. ISBN 81-8356-305-8 (set).

Ediger, Marlow and Digumarti Bhaskara Rao, Editors (2007). *Encyclopaedia of Teaching,* 8 volumes. New Delhi: Discovery Publishing House. ISBN 81-8356-305-8 (set).

Marlow Ediger and Digumarti Bhaskara Rao, Editors (2006). *Encyclopaedia of School Education,* 5 volumes. New Delhi: Discovery Publishing House. ISBN 81-8356-308-2 (set).

Marlow Ediger and Digumarti Bhaskara Rao, Editors (2006). *Encyclopaedia of School Administration,* 4 volumes. New Delhi: Discovery Publishing House. ISBN 81-8356-307-4 (set).

Marlow Ediger and Digumarti Bhaskara Rao, Editors (2007). *Encyclopaedia of School Curriculum,* 10 volumes. New Delhi: Discovery Publishing House. ISBN 81-8356-305-8 (set).

Marlow Ediger and Digumarti Bhaskara Rao, Editors (2007). *Encyclopaedia of Teaching,* 8 volumes. New Delhi: Discovery Publishing House. ISBN 81-8356-305-8 (set).

Ediger, Marlow and Digumarti Bhaskara Rao (1996). *Science Curriculum.* New Delhi: Discovery Publishing House. ISBN 81-7141-321-8.

Ediger, Marlow and Digumarti Bhaskara Rao (2000). *Teaching Mathematics Successfully.* New Delhi: Discovery Publishing House. ISBN 81-7141-552-0.

Ediger, Marlow and Digumarti Bhaskara Rao (2001). *Teaching Science Successfully.* New Delhi: Discovery Publishing House. ISBN 81-7141-600-4.

Ediger, Marlow and Digumarti Bhaskara Rao (2001). *Teaching Social Studies Successfully.* New Delhi: Discovery Publishing House. ISBN 81-7141-596-2.

Ediger, Marlow and Digumarti Bhaskara Rao (2002). *Philosophy and Curriculum.* New Delhi: Discovery Publishing House. ISBN 81-7141-631-4.

Ediger, Marlow and Digumarti Bhaskara Rao (2002). *Improving School Administration.* New Delhi: Discovery Publishing House. ISBN 81-7141-633-0

Ediger, Marlow and Digumarti Bhaskara Rao (2002). *Elementary Curriculum.* New Delhi: Discovery Publishing House. ISBN 81-7141-658-6.

Ediger, Marlow and Digumarti Bhaskara Rao (2003). *Language Arts Curriculum.* New Delhi: Discovery Publishing House. ISBN 81-7141-657-8.

Ediger, Marlow and Digumarti Bhaskara Rao (2003). *Psychology and Curriculum.* New Delhi: Discovery Publishing House. ISBN 81-7141-691-8.

Ediger, Marlow and Digumarti Bhaskara Rao (2003). *Teaching Language Arts Successfully.* New Delhi: Discovery Publishing House. ISBN 81-7141-678-0.

Ediger, Marlow and Digumarti Bhaskara Rao (2003). *School Curriculum and Administration.* New Delhi: Discovery Publishing House. ISBN 81-7141-709-4.

Ediger, Marlow and Digumarti Bhaskara Rao (2003). *Teaching Mathematics in Elementary Schools*. New Delhi: Discovery Publishing House. ISBN 81-7141-687-X.

Ediger, Marlow and Digumarti Bhaskara Rao (2003). *Teaching Science in Elementary Schools*. New Delhi: Discovery Publishing House. ISBN 81-7141-698-5.

Ediger, Marlow and Digumarti Bhaskara Rao (2003). *School Curriculum and Administration*. New Delhi: Discovery Publishing House. ISBN 81-7141-709-4.

Ediger, Marlow and Digumarti Bhaskara Rao (2003). *Elementary Curriculum Improvement*. New Delhi: Discovery Publishing House. ISBN 81-7141-740-X.

Ediger, Marlow and Digumarti Bhaskara Rao (2004). *School Organisation*. New Delhi: Discovery Publishing House. ISBN 81-7141-843-0.

Ediger, Marlow and Digumarti Bhaskara Rao (2004). *Relevancy in Elementary Curriculum*. New Delhi: Discovery Publishing House. ISBN 81-7141-845-9.

Ediger, Marlow and Digumarti Bhaskara Rao (2005). *Quality School Education*. New Delhi: Discovery Publishing House. ISBN 81-8356-022-9.

Ediger, Marlow and Digumarti Bhaskara Rao (2006). *Successful School Education*. New Delhi: Discovery Publishing House. ISBN 81-8356-054-7.

Ediger, Marlow and Digumarti Bhaskara Rao (2006). *Successful School Administration*. New Delhi: Discovery Publishing House. ISBN 81-8356-046-6.

Ediger, Marlow and Digumarti Bhaskara Rao (2006). *Issues in School Curruculum*. New Delhi: Discovery Publishing House. ISBN 81-8356-052-0.

Ediger, Marlow and Digumarti Bhaskara Rao (2006). *Community College — Curriculum and Teaching*. New Delhi: Discovery Publishing House. ISBN 81-8356-053-9.

Ediger, Marlow and Digumarti Bhaskara Rao (2006). *Administration of Schools*. New Delhi: Discovery Publishing House. ISBN 81-8356-244-2.

Ediger, Marlow and Digumarti Bhaskara Rao (2006). *Reading Curriculum and Instruction*. New Delhi: Discovery Publishing House. ISBN 81-8356-266-3.

Ediger, Marlow and Digumarti Bhaskara Rao (2006). *Curriculum Organisation*. New Delhi: Discovery Publishing House. ISBN 81-8356-205-1.

Ediger, Marlow and Digumarti Bhaskara Rao (2006). *Curriculum of School Subjects*. New Delhi: Discovery Publishing House. ISBN 81-8356-207-8.

Ediger, Marlow, B.S.V. Dutt and Digumarti Bhaskara Rao (2003). *Teaching English Successfully*. New Delhi: Discovery Publishing House. ISBN 81-7141-707-8.

Ediger, Marlow and Digumarti Bhaskara Rao (2007). *School Science Education*. New Delhi: Discovery Publishing House. ISBN 81-8356-352-X.

Ediger, Marlow and Digumarti Bhaskara Rao (2007). *Language Arts Education*. New Delhi: Discovery Publishing House. ISBN 81-8356-333-3.

Ediger, Marlow and Digumarti Bhaskara Rao (2010). *Effective Schooling*. New Delhi: Discovery Publishing House. ISBN 978-81-8356-613-1.

Ediger, Marlow and Digumarti Bhaskara Rao (2010). *Effective School Curriculum*. New Delhi: Discovery Publishing House. ISBN 978-81-8356-585-1.

Ediger, Marlow and Digumarti Bhaskara Rao (2010). *Essays on Teaching Science*. New Delhi: Discovery Publishing House. ISBN 978-81-8356-882-1.

Ediger, Marlow and Digumarti Bhaskara Rao (2010). *Essays on Teaching Social Studies*. New Delhi: Discovery Publishing House. ISBN 978-81-8356-883-8.

Ediger, Marlow and Digumarti Bhaskara Rao (2010). *Essays on Teaching Reading*. New Delhi: Discovery Publishing House. ISBN 978-81-8356-881-4.

Ediger, Marlow and Digumarti Bhaskara Rao (2010). *Essays on Teaching Mathematics*. New Delhi: Discovery Publishing House. ISBN 978-81-8356-880-7.

Elizabeth, M.E.S., Author and Digumarti Bhaskara Rao, Editor (2004). *Methods of Teaching English*. New Delhi: Discovery Publishing House. ISBN 81-7141-809-0.

Elizabeth, M.E.S., Author and Digumarti Bhaskara Rao, Editor (2004). *Acquisition of English Vocabulary*. New Delhi: Discovery Publishing House. ISBN 81-8356-075-X.

Fatima, Sk. Author and Digumarti Bhaskara Rao, Editor (2007). *Reasoning Ability of School Students*. New Delhi: Discovery Publishing House. ISBN 81-8356-330-9.

Fatima, Sk. and Digumarti Bhaskara Rao (2008). *Reasoning Ability of Adolescent Students*. New Delhi: Discovery Publishing House. ISBN 978-81-8356-315-4.

Gopala Krishna, M., Author and Digumarti Bhaskara Rao, Editor (2007). *Techniques of Teaching Physical Education*. New Delhi: Sonali Publications. ISBN 81-8411-044-8.

Gopala Krishna, M., Author and Digumarti Bhaskara Rao, Editor (2007). *Techniques of Teaching Education*. New Delhi: Sonali Publications. ISBN 81-8411-062-6.

Harshitha, Digumarthi, Author and Digumarti Bhaskara Rao, Editor (2004). *Methods of Teaching Information Technology*. New Delhi: Discovery Publishing House. ISBN 81-7141-805-8.

Harshitha, Digumarthi, Author and Digumarti Bhaskara Rao, Editor (2007). *Techniques of Teaching Computer Science*. New Delhi: Sonali Publications. ISBN 81-8411-036-7.

Indira Devi, Author and J. Prasanth Kumar and Digumarti Bhaskara Rao, Editors (2004). *Values in Language Text Books*. New Delhi: Discovery Publishing House. ISBN 81-7141-833-3.

Jalaja Kumari, C., Author and Digumarti Bhaskara Rao, Editor (2004). *Methods of Teaching Educational Technology*. New Delhi: Discovery Publishing House. ISBN 81-7141-810-4.

Jalaja Kumari, C., Author and Digumarti Bhaskara Rao, Editor (2007). *Job Satisfaction of Teachers*. New Delhi: Discovery Publishing House. ISBN 81-8356-329-5.

Janardhan Reddy, B., Author and Digumarti Bhaskara Rao, Editor (2006). *Techniques of Teaching Sociology*. New Delhi: Sonali Publications. ISBN 81-8411-042-1.

Jayasree, K., Author and Digumarti Bhaskara Rao, Editor (1999). *Correlates of Socialisation*. New Delhi: Discovery Publishing House. ISBN 81-7141-517-2.

Jayasree, K., Author and Digumarti Bhaskara Rao, Editor (2004). *Methods of Teaching Science*. New Delhi: Discovery Publishing House. ISBN 81-7141-801-5.

John Babu, C., Author and T.J.R. Prasad, G.M. Madhukar and Digumarti Bhaskara Rao, Editors (2004). *Problem Solving in Mathematics*. New Delhi: APH Publishing Corporation. ISBN 81-7648-273-0.

Joseph Raju, B and G.A. Anitha, Authors and Digumarti Bhaskara Rao, Editor (2004). *Population Education*. New Delhi: Sonali Publications. ISBN 81-88836-31-3.

Lalitha, T., Author and K.S. Prabhakaram, D.S.N. Sastry and Digumarti Bhaskara Rao, Editors (2004). *Educational Philosophic Beliefs*. New Delhi: Discovery Publishing House. ISBN 81-7141-765-5.

Krishna, G., Author and Digumarti Bhaskara Rao, Editor (2006). *Techniques of Teaching Physical Education*. New Delhi: Sonali Publications. ISBN 81-8411-044-8.

Kumar Raja, G., Author and Digumarti Bhaskara Rao, Editor (2007). *Principles of Primary School*. New Delhi: Sonali Publications. ISBN 81-8411-054-5.

Lakshmi Kumari, V., Author and Digumarti Bhaskara Rao, Editor (2006). *Techniques of Teaching Home Science*. New Delhi: Sonali Publications. ISBN 81-8411-048-0.

Madhava, K., Author and Digumarti Bhaskara Rao, Editor (2008). *Personality of Adolescent Students.* New Delhi: Discovery Publishing House. ISBN 978-81-8356-262-1.

Madhu Bala, Jampala, Author and Digumarti Bhaskara Rao, Editor (2004). *Methods of Teaching Exceptional Children.* New Delhi: Discovery Publishing House. ISBN 81-7141-802-3.

Mallikarjuna Reddy, V., Author and Digumarti Bhaskara Rao, Editor (2011). *Teaching Aptitude, Social Adjustment and Job Satisfaction of Science Teachers.* New Delhi: Discovery Publishing House.

Marja, Talvi and Digumarti Bhaskara Rao, Editors (1996). *Educational Leadership and Social Changes.* New Delhi: Discovery Publishing House. ISBN 81-7141-320-X.

Naga Kumari, U., Author and Digumarti Bhaskara Rao, Editor (2008). *Science Process Skills of School Students.* New Delhi: Sonali Publications. ISBN 978-81-8356-263-8.

Nageswara Rao, S. and M. Srihari, Authors and Digumarti Bhaskara Rao, Editor (2004). *Guidance and Counselling.* New Delhi: Discovery Publishing House. ISBN 81-7141-840-6.

Nageswara Rao, S., Author and Digumarti Bhaskara Rao, Editor (2006). *Techniques of Teaching Psychology.* New Delhi: Discovery Publishing House. ISBN 81-8411-040-5.

Nageswara Rao, S. and P. Sridhar, Authors and Digumarti Bhaskara Rao, Editor (2004). *Methods and Techniques of Teaching.* New Delhi: Sonali Publications. ISBN 81-88836-33-8.

Nirmala Jyothi, M., Author and Digumarti Bhaskara Rao, Editor (2003). *Non-detention System in School Education.* New Delhi: Discovery Publishing House. ISBN 81-7141-654-3.

Padma Tulasi, G., Author and Digumarti Bhaskara Rao, Editor (2004). *Methods of Teaching Elementary Science.* New Delhi: Discovery Publishing House. ISBN 81-7141-871-6.

Pala Prasada Rao, V., Author and K. N. Rani and D. Bhaskara Rao, Editors (2004).*India Pakistan: Partition Perspectives in Indo English Novels.* New Delhi: Discovery Publishing House. ISBN 81-7141-871-6.

Pala Prasada Rao, V., Author and D. Bhaskara Rao, Editors (2008). *Functioning of Autonomous Colleges.* New Delhi: Sonali Publications. ISBN 978-81-8356-258-4.

Pitchi Reddy, M., Author and Digumarti Bhaskara Rao, Editor (2007). *Techniques of Teaching Social Sciences.* New Delhi: Sonali Publications. ISBN 81-8411-066-X.

Prasad Babu, B., Author and P. Madhu and Digumarti Bhaskara Rao, Editors (2006). *Psychological Adjustment and Well-being.* New Delhi: Discovery Publishing House. ISBN 81-8356-204-3.

Prasad Babu, B., Author and M.V.R. Raju and Digumarti Bhaskara Rao, Editors (2006). *Behavioural Problems of School Children.* New Delhi: Discovery Publishing House. ISBN 81-8356-206-X.

Prabhakaram, K.S., Author and Digumarti Bhaskara Rao, Editors (1998). *Concept Attainment Model in Mathematics Teaching.* New Delhi: Discovery Publishing House. ISBN 81-7141-424-9.

Prasanth Kumar, J., Author and Digumarti Bhaskara Rao, Editor (1998). *Effectiveness of Distance Education System.* New Delhi: Discovery Publishing House. ISBN 81-7141-437-0.

Prasanth Kumar, J., Author and Digumarti Bhaskara Rao, Editor (2004). *Methods of Teaching Civics.* New Delhi: Discovery Publishing House. ISBN 81-7141-806-6.

Prasanth Kumar, J., Author and G. Sundara Rao and Digumarti Bhaskara Rao, Editors (2000). *Open University Student Support Services.* New Delhi: Discovery Publishing House. ISBN 81-7141-550-4.

Raja Kumari, M.A. and D.R.S. Sundari, Authors and Digumarti Bhaskara Rao, Editor (2004). *Special Education.* New Delhi: Discovery Publishing House. ISBN 81-7141-846-5.

Raja Kumari, M.A. and D.R.S. Sundari, Authors and Digumarti Bhaskara Rao, Editor (2004). *Methods of Teaching Educational Psychology.* New Delhi: Discovery Publishing House. ISBN 81-7141-820-1.

Ramatulasamma, K., Author and Digumarti Bhaskara Rao, Editor (2002). *Job Satisfaction of Teacher Educators.* New Delhi: Discovery Publishing House. ISBN 81-7141-655-1.

Rama Krishnaiah, D., Author and Digumarti Bhaskara Rao, Editor (1998). *Job Satisfaction of College Teachers.* New Delhi: Discovery Publishing House. ISBN 81-7141-438-9.

Rama Kumar Ratnam, M.V., Author and Digumarti Bhaskara Rao, Editor (1998). *Dukkha: Suffering in Early Buddhism.* New Delhi: Discovery Publishing House. ISBN 81-7141-653-5.

Rama Krishna Prasad and P. Vide Sagar, Authors and Digumarti Bhaskara Rao, Editor (2004). *Methods of Teaching Physical Education.* New Delhi: Discovery Publishing House. ISBN 81-7141-868-6.

Rama Seshaiah, P. Author and Digumarti Bhaskara Rao, Editor (2004). *Methods of Teaching Home Science.* New Delhi: Discovery Publishing House. ISBN 81-7141-916-X.

Rama Swamy, K., Author and Digumarti Bhaskara Rao, Editor (2007). *Techniques of Teaching Environmental Science.* New Delhi: Sonali Publications. ISBN 81-8411-035-9.

Ramesh, A.R., Author and Digumarti Bhaskara Rao, Editor (2006). *Techniques of Teaching Commerce.* New Delhi: Sonali Publications. ISBN 81-8411-043-X.

Ramesh, Ghanta and Digumarti Bhaskara Rao, Editors (1998). *Environmental Education: Problems and Prospects.* New Delhi: Discovery Publishing House. ISBN 81-7141-423-0.

Ranga Rao, B., Author and Digumarti Bhaskara Rao, Editor (2007). *Techniques of Teaching Economics*. New Delhi: Sonali Publications. ISBN 81-8411-056-1.

Ranga Rao, R., Author and Digumarti Bhaskara Rao, Editor (2004). *Methods of Teacher Teaching*. New Delhi: Discovery Publishing House. ISBN 81-7141-812-0.

Rani, S.S., Author and Digumarti Bhaskara Rao, Editor (2006). *Techniques of Teaching Botany*. New Delhi: Sonali Publications. ISBN 81-8411-037-5.

Rathaiah, Lavu and Digumarti Bhaskara Rao, Editors (1996), *International Innovations in Education*. New Delhi: Discovery Publishing House. ISBN 81-7141-359-5.

Rathaiah, Lavu and Digumarti Bhaskara Rao (1997). *Achievement Correlates*. New Delhi: Discovery Publishing House. ISBN 81-7141-385-4.

Ravi Krishna, M., Author and Digumarti Bhaskara Rao, Editor (2004). *Examination System*. New Delhi: Discovery Publishing House. ISBN 81-7141-824-4.

Ravi Kumar, M., Author and Digumarti Bhaskara Rao, Editor (2004). *Methods of Teaching Computer Science*. New Delhi: Discovery Publishing House. ISBN 81-7141-823-6.

Rudramamba, B., Author and Digumarti Bhaskara Rao, Editor (2003). *Problems of Teaching*. New Delhi: APH Publishing Corporation. ISBN 81-7648-462-8.

Rudramamba, B. and V. Lakshmi Kumari, Authors and Digumarti Bhaskara Rao, Editor (2004). *Methods of Teaching Economics*. New Delhi: Discovery Publishing House. ISBN 81-7141-900-3.

Sambasiva Rao, P., Author and Digumarti Bhaskara Rao, Editor (2007). *Techniques of Teaching Psychology*. New Delhi: Sonali Publications. ISBN 81-8411-040-5.

Sanjeeva Rao, P.C., Author and Digumarti Bhaskara Rao, Editor (1996). *A Text Book of Geology*. New Delhi: Discovery Publishing House. ISBN 81-7141-313-7.

Santhanam, T., B. Prasad Babu and S. Sugandhi, Authors and Digumarti Bhaskara Rao, Editor (2007). *Children with Learning Disabilities.* New Delhi: Sonali Publications. ISBN 81-8411-077-4.

Santhanam, T., B. Prasad Babu and S. Sugandhi, Authors and Digumarti Bhaskara Rao, Editor (2008). *Learning Disabilities and Remedial Programmes.* New Delhi: Discovery Publishing House. ISBN 978-81-8356-257-7.

Sarala, M.M.O., Author and Digumarti Bhaskara Rao, Editor (2006). *Techniques of Teaching English.* New Delhi: Sonali Publications. ISBN 81-8411-047-2.

Satya Narayana, G., Author and Digumarti Bhaskara Rao, Editor (2008). *Attitude Towards Social Studies and Achievement in Social Studies.* New Delhi: Discovery Publishing House. ISBN 978-81-8356-261-4.

Satya Narayana, V., Author and Digumarti Bhaskara Rao, Editor (2001). *Physical Education, Social Attitudes and Leadership Qualities.* New Delhi: Discovery Publishing House. ISBN 81-7141-593-8.

Satya Narayana, P.V.V. and G. Krishna, Authors and Digumarti Bhaskara Rao, Editor (2004). *Curriculum Development and Management.* New Delhi: Discovery Publishing House. ISBN 81-7141-813-9.

Shamsuddin, Sk. and V. Dayakara Reddy, Authors and Digumarti Bhaskara Rao, Editor (2007). *Values and Academic Achievement.* New Delhi: Discovery Publishing House. ISBN 81-8356-283-3.

Singh, Y.C., Author and Digumarti Bhaskara Rao, Editor (2006). *Techniques of Teaching Science.* New Delhi: Sonali Publications. ISBN 81-8411-041-3.

Sirisha Rani, S., Author and Digumarti Bhaskara Rao, Editor (2007). *Techniques of Teaching Botany.* New Delhi: Sonali Publications. ISBN 81-8411-037-5.

Sivaratnam Reddy, M., Author and Digumarti Bhaskara Rao, Editor (2004). *Creativity in College Students.* New Delhi: Discovery Publishing House. ISBN 81-7141-697-7.

Siva Lakshmi, G.V. and G.L. Subbaiah, Authors and Digumarti Bhaskara Rao, Editor (2004). *Methods of Teaching Environmental Science.* New Delhi: Discovery Publishing House. ISBN 81-7141-839-2.

Srinivas, G. and Digumarti Bhaskara Rao (2007). *Anxiety of Prospective Teachers.* New Delhi: Sonali Publications. ISBN 81-8411-084-7.

Srinivas, G. and Digumarti Bhaskara Rao (2011). *Intelligence and Personality of Prospective Teachers.* New Delhi: Discovery Publishing House. ISBN

Srinivas, M. and I. Prasada Rao, Authors and Digumarti Bhaskara Rao, Editor (2004). *Methods of Teaching History.* New Delhi: Discovery Publishing House. ISBN 81-7141-803-1

Srinivas Rao, P., Author and Digumarti Bhaskara Rao, Editor (2007). *Principles of Secondary School.* New Delhi: Sonali Publications. ISBN 81-8411-058-8.

Srinivasulu, K., Author and Digumarti Bhaskara Rao, Editor (2011). *Achievement Motivation and Academic Achievement of Alcoholic and Non-alcoholic College Students.* New Delhi: Discovery Publishing House Pvt. Ltd.

Srinivasulu Reddy, M. and K.R.S. Sambasiva Rao, Authors and Digumarti Bhaskara Rao, Editor (1999). *A Text Book of Aquaculture.* New Delhi: Discovery Publishing House. ISBN 81-7141-482-6.

Srinivasa Rao, Mandalapu, Author and Digumarti Bhaskara Rao, Editor (2003). *Achievement Motivation and Achievement in Mathematics.* New Delhi: Discovery Publishing House. ISBN 81-7141-674-8.

Srihari, M., Author and Digumarti Bhaskara Rao, Editor (2003). *Values of Prospective Teachers.* New Delhi: Discovery Publishing House. ISBN 81-8356-328-7.

Subba Rao, K., Author and Digumarti Bhaskara Rao, Editor (2007). *School Education Policy.* New Delhi: Discovery Publishing House. ISBN 81-8356-285-X.

Subba Rao, K., Author and Digumarti Bhaskara Rao, Editor (2007). *Education Planning*. New Delhi: Sonali Publications. ISBN 81-8411-053-7.

Subramanyam, N.R., Author and Digumarti Bhaskara Rao, Editor (2011). *Effectiveness of In-service Training Programmes*. New Delhi: Discovery Publishing House.

Sudhakar Reddy, Y., Author and Digumarti Bhaskara Rao, Editor (2003). *Creativity in Adolescents*. New Delhi: Discovery Publishing House. ISBN 81-7141-659-4.

Sunil Kumar, K. and K. Rama Krishana, Authors and Digumarti Bhaskara Rao, Editor (2004). *Methods of Teaching Chemistry*. New Delhi: Discovery Publishing House. ISBN 81-7141-913-5.

Suneetha, G., Author and Digumarti Bhaskara Rao, Editor (2004). *Environmental Awareness of School Students*. New Delhi: Sonali Publications. ISBN 81-8411-085-5.

Sunita, E. and R. Sambasiva Rao, Authors and Digumarti Bhaskara Rao, Editor (2004). *Methods of Teaching Mathematics*. New Delhi: Discovery Publishing House. ISBN 81-7141-915-1.

Surya Madhava, I., Author and Digumarti Bhaskara Rao, Editor (2006). *Techniques of Teaching Geography*. New Delhi: Sonali Publications. ISBN 81-8411-034-0.

Surya Madhava, I., Author and Digumarti Bhaskara Rao, Editor (2007). *Techniques of Teaching Political Science*. New Delhi: Sonali Publications. ISBN 81-8411-061-8.

Swamy, K.R., Author and Digumarti Bhaskara Rao, Editor (2006). *Techniques of Teaching Environmental Science*. New Delhi: Sonali Publications. ISBN 81-8411-035-9.

Swarna Jyothi, K., Author and Digumarti Bhaskara Rao, Editor (2007). *Educational Research*. New Delhi: Sonali Publications. ISBN 81-8411-063-4.

Swarna Latha, C.D., and Digumarti Bhaskara Rao, Editors (2006). *Encyclopaedia of Biotechnology*, 5 volumes. New Delhi: Discovery Publishing House. ISBN 81-8356-168-3.

Swarupa Rani, T. and J.R. Priyadarshini, Authors and Digumarti Bhaskara Rao, Editor (2004). *Educational Measurement and Evaluation.* New Delhi: Discovery Publishing House. ISBN 81-7141-859-7.

Vanaja, M., Author and Digumarti Bhaskara Rao, Editor (1999). *Inquiry Training Model.* New Delhi: Discovery Publishing House. ISBN 81-7141-515-6.

Vanaja, M., Author and Digumarti Bhaskara Rao, Editor (2004). *Methods of Teaching Physics.* New Delhi: Discovery Publishing House. ISBN 81-7141-867-8.

Valeri V. Koustiouk, Author and Digumarti Bhaskara Rao, Editor (2002). *A Text Book of Cryogenics.* New Delhi: Discovery Publishing House. ISBN 81-7141-642-X.

Vamsi Krishna, V., Author and Digumarti Bhaskara Rao, Editor (2004). *School Psychology.* New Delhi: Discovery Publishing House. ISBN 81-7141-880-5.

Veena Kumari, Balusu and Digumarti Bhaskara Rao (1996). *Operation Black Board.* New Delhi: Discovery Publishing House. ISBN 81-8356-354-6.

Veena Kumari, Balusu, Author and Digumarti Bhaskara Rao, Editor (2004). *Methods of Teaching Social Studies.* New Delhi: Discovery Publishing House. ISBN 81-7141-899-6.

Veena Kumari, Balusu, Author and Digumarti Bhaskara Rao, Editor (2000). *Psycho-social Correlates of Achievement.* New Delhi: Discovery Publishing House. ISBN 81-7141-547-4.

Venkata Rao, B., Author and Digumarti Bhaskara Rao, Editor (2007). *Techniques of Teaching Chemistry.* New Delhi: Sonali Publications. ISBN 81-8411-057-X.

Venkata Rao, P. and Digumarti Bhaskara Rao (1989). **A** *Text Book of Zoology — Junior Intermediate.* Guntur: Vignan Publishers.

Venkata Rao, P. and Digumarti Bhaskara Rao (1989). **A** *Text Book of Zoology — Senior Intermediate.* Guntur: Vignan Publishers.

Venkateswara Rao, V., Author and Digumarti Bhaskara Rao, Editor (2004). *Problems of Education.* New Delhi: Discovery Publishing House. ISBN 81-7141-841-4.

Venkateswara Rao, V., V. Vijaya Lakshmi and V. Vamsi Krishna, Authors and Digumarti Bhaskara Rao, Editor (2004). *Education For All.* New Delhi: Sonali Publications. ISBN 81-88836-30-3.

Venkateswara Rao, V., V. Vijaya Lakshmi and V. Vamsi Krishna, Authors and Digumarti Bhaskara Rao, Editor (2004). *Education in India.* New Delhi: Sonali Publications. ISBN 81-88836-858-9.

Venkateswara Reddy, L. and Narayana, M. L., Authors and Digumarti Bhaskara Rao, Editor (2004). *Education for Dalits.* New Delhi: Discovery Publishing House. ISBN 81-7141-872-4.

Venkateswara Reddy, L. and Narayana, M. L, Authors and Digumarti Bhaskara Rao, Editor (2004). *Methods of Teaching Rural Sociology.* New Delhi: Discovery Publishing House. ISBN 81-7141-811-2.

Venkateswarlu, K. and S.J. Basha, Authors and Digumarti Bhaskara Rao, Editor (2004). *Methods of Teaching Commerce.* New Delhi: Discovery Publishing House. ISBN 81-7141-808-2.

Venugopala Rao, K., Author and Digumarti Bhaskara Rao, Editor (2000). *Teacher Morale in Secondary Schools.* New Delhi: Discovery Publishing House. ISBN 81-7141-551-2.

Venugopala Rao, K., Author and Digumarti Bhaskara Rao, Editor (2007). *Techniques of Teaching History.* New Delhi: Sonali Publications. ISBN 81-8411-059-6.

Vidya, C., Author and Digumarti Bhaskara Rao, Editor (1996). *A Text Book of Nutrition.* New Delhi: Discovery Publishing House. ISBN 81-7141-309-9.

Vimala, T.D., B. Prasad Babu and Digumarti Bhaskara Rao, Editors (2007). *Stress, Coping and Management.* New Delhi: Sonali Publications. ISBN 81-8411-086-3.

Vijaya Bharathi, D., Author and Digumarti Bhaskara Rao, Editor (2000). *Educational Philosophies of Swami Vivekananda and John Dewey.* New Delhi: APH Publishing House. ISBN 81-7648-309-9.

Vijaya Bharathi, D., Author and Digumarti Bhaskara Rao, Editor (2005). *Educational Philosophy of John Dewey.* New Delhi: Discovery Publishing House. ISBN 81-8356-024-5.

Vijaya Bharathi, D., Author and Digumarti Bhaskara Rao, Editor (2005). *Educational Philosophy of Swami Vivekananda.* New Delhi: Discovery Publishing House. ISBN 81-8356-023-7.

Vijaya Lakshmi, D., Author and Digumarti Bhaskara Rao, Editor (2004) *Basic Education.* New Delhi: Discovery Publishing House. ISBN 81-7141-881-3.

Vijaya Lakshmi, V., Author and Digumarti Bhaskara Rao, Editor (2006). *Techniques of Teaching Music.* New Delhi: Discovery Publishing House. ISBN 81-8411-038-3.

Vijaya Kumar, S.J., Author and Digumarti Bhaskara Rao, Editor (2006). *Techniques of Teaching Mathematics.* New Delhi: Sonali Publications. ISBN 81-8411-039-1.

Visalakshi, V., Author and Digumarti Bhaskara Rao, Editor (2006). *Techniques of Teaching Biology.* New Delhi: Sonali Publications. ISBN 81-8411-045-6.

Visalakshi, V., Author and Digumarti Bhaskara Rao, Editor (2007). *Techniques of Teaching Zoology.* New Delhi: Sonali Publications. ISBN 81-8411-055-3.

Books in Telugu Language

Bhaskara Rao, Digumarti (1986). *Dhrushya Sravana Bodhanapakaranalu* (Audio-visual Teaching Aids). Guntur: Nagarjuna Publishers.

Bhaskara Rao, Digumarti (1993). *Jeevasashtra Bodhana* (Teaching of Biology). Guntur: Nagarjuna Publishers.

Bhaskara Rao, Digumarti (1995). *Vignanasasthra Bodhana* (Teaching of science) Guntur: Nagarjuna Publishers.

Bhaskara Rao, Digumarti (1994). *Vidya Manovignana Sastram* (Educational Psychology). Guntur: Nagarjuna Publishers.

Bhaskara Rao, Digumarti (1997). *Vidya Manovignana Sastram* (Educational Psychology). Guntur: Creative Press.

Bhaskara Rao, Digumarti (1998). *DSC Study Material*. Guntur: Nagarjuna Publishers.

Bhaskara Rao, Digumarti (1998). *Upadhyayudu Vidya*. (Teacher and Education) Guntur: Nagarjuna Publishers.

Bhaskara Rao, Digumarti (1998). *Vidya Drukpadalu* (Perspectives of Education). Guntur: Nagarjuna Publishers.

Bhaskara Rao, Digumarti (1999). *EdCET Teaching Aptitude*. Guntur: Nagarjuna Publishers.

Bhaskara Rao, Digumarti (2001). *Bharata Samajamulo Upadyayudu Vidhya* (Teacher and Education in Emerging Indian Society). Guntur: Sri Nagarjuna Publishers.

Bhaskara Rao, Digumarti (2001). *Bhoutika Sastra Bodhana Padhatulu* (Methods of Teaching Physical Science). Guntur: Sri Nagarjuna Publishers.

Bhaskara Rao, Digumarti (2001). *Jeeva Sastra Bodhana Padhatulu* (Methods of Teaching Biology).Guntur: Sri Nagarjuna Publishers.

Bhaskara Rao, Digumarti (2001). *Vidya Manovignana Sastram* (Educational Psychology). Guntur: Sri Nagarjuna Publishers.

Bhaskara Rao, Digumarti (2003). *Patasala Yajamanyam/ Paripalana* (School Management and Administration). Guntur: Sri Nagarjuna Publishers.

Bhaskara Rao, Digumarti and M. Srihari (2009). *Vardamana Bharata Desamulo Vidya* (Education in Emerging India). Guntur: Sri Nagarjuna Publishers.

Bhaskara Rao, Digumarti and B. Prasad Babu (2009). *Vidya Manovignana Sastram* (Educational Psychology). Guntur: Sri Nagarjuna Publishers.

Bhaskara Rao, Digumarti and B. Prasad Babu (2009). *Pradhamika Vidya mariyu Vileena Vidya Dhrukpadhalu* (Perspectives in Primary Education and Inclusive Education). Guntur: Sri Nagarjuna Publishers.

Bhaskara Rao, Digumarti and K. Subba Rao (2009). *Elementary Vidya, Pranalika, Yajamanyam, Upadyaya Kartavyalu* (Elementary Education, Planning, Management and Teacher Functions). Guntur: Sri Nagarjuna Publishers.

Bhaskara Rao, Digumarti and G. Prasanthi (2009). *Samardya Nirmanamu* (Capacity Building). Guntur: Sri Nagarjuna Publishers.

Bhaskara Rao, Digumarti and A. Jagadish (2009). *Vignansastra Bodhana Padhatulu* (Methods of Teaching Science). Guntur: Sri Nagarjuna Publishers.

Bhaskara Rao, Digumarti, Editor (2010). *Vardamana Bharata Desamulo Vidya — Question Bank* (Education in Emerging India). Guntur: Sri Nagarjuna Publishers.

Bhaskara Rao, Digumarti, Editor (2010). *Vidya Manovignana Sastram — Question Bank* (Educational Psychology). Guntur: Sri Nagarjuna Publishers.

Bhaskara Rao, Digumarti, Editor (2010). *Pradhamika Vidya mariyu Vileena Vidya Dhrukpadhalu — Question Bank* (Perspectives in Primary Education and Inclusive Education). Guntur: Sri Nagarjuna Publishers.

Bhaskara Rao, Digumarti, Editor (2010). *Elementary Vidya, Pranalika, Yajamanyam, Upadyaya Kartavyalu — Question Bank* (Elementary Education, Planning, Management and Teacher Functions). Guntur: Sri Nagarjuna Publishers.

Bhaskara Rao, Digumarti, Editor (2010). *Samardya Nirmanamu — Question Bank* (Capacity Building). Guntur: Sri Nagarjuna Publishers.

Bhaskara Rao, Digumarti, Editor (2010). *Ganithasastra Bodhana Padhatulu — Question Bank* (Methods of Teaching Science).Guntur: Sri Nagarjuna Publishers.

Bhaskara Rao, Digumarti, Editor (2010). *Vignansastra Bodhana Padhatulu — Question Bank* (Methods of Teaching Science).Guntur: Sri Nagarjuna Publishers.

Bhaskara Rao, Digumarti, Editor (2010). *Sanghikasastra Bodhana Padhatulu — Question Bank* (Methods of Teaching Social Studies).Guntur: Sri Nagarjuna Publishers.

Bhaskara Rao, Digumarti, Editor (2010). *Telugu Bodhana Padhatulu — Question Bank* (Methods of Teaching Social Studies).Guntur: Sri Nagarjuna Publishers.

Bhaskara Rao, Digumarti, Editor (2010). *Methods of Teaching English — Question Bank*. Guntur: Sri Nagarjuna Publishers.

Bhaskara Rao, Digumarti, N. Saraja, J. Lalitha and V. Mrunalini, Translators (2008). *Vidya — Samajam (Education - Society). Hyderabad:* Dr. B. R. Ambedkar Open University.

Gopala Krishna, G., A. Rama Krishna, K. Subba Rao and Bhaskara Rao, Digumarti (2004). *Jeevasashtra Bodhana Padhatulu* (Methods of Teaching of Biological science). Guntur: Sri Nagarjuna Publishers.

Krishna Murthy, V., K.S. Sudheer Reddy and Digumarti Bhaskara Rao (2004). *Vidya Manovignana Sastra Adharalu* (Foundations of Educational Psychology). Guntur: Sri Nagarjuna Publishers.

Lalini, V., V. Dayakara Reddy, M. Srihari and Digumarti Bhaskara Rao (2004). *Vidya Adharalu* (Foundations of Education). Guntur: Sri Nagarjuna Publishers.

Sastry, G.E.P. and G. Satya Narayana, Authors, Bhaskara Rao, Digumarti, Editor (2009). *Sanghikasastra Bodhana Padhatulu* (Methods of Teaching Social Studies).Guntur: Sri Nagarjuna Publishers.

Subba Rao, K.P., P. Ayodhya and Digumarti Bhaskara Rao (2004). *Patasala Yajamanyam — Vidhya Vyavasthalu* (School Management and Systems of Education). Guntur: Sri Nagarjuna Publishers.

Sudhakar, V., B. Ravindra Babu, D.S. Kumar and Digumarti Bhaskara Rao (2004). *Vidya Sanketika Sastram - Computer Vidhya* (Educational Technology and Computer Education). Guntur: Sri Nagarjuna Publishers.

Index